M000219953

How to
Be Free
from the
Fear of
Death

RAY COMFORT

BroadStreet
PUBLISHING

BroadStreet Publishing® Group, LLC
Savage, Minnesota, USA
BroadStreetPublishing.com

How to Be Free from the Fear of Death
Copyright © 2021 Ray Comfort

978-1-4245-6281-7 (faux)
978-1-4245-6282-4 (e-book)

All rights reserved. No part of this book may be reproduced in any form, except for brief quotations in printed reviews, without permission in writing from the publisher.

Unless otherwise indicated, Scripture quotations are taken from the New King James Version®. Copyright © 1982 by Thomas Nelson. Used by permission. All rights reserved. Scripture marked KJV is taken from the King James Version of the Bible, public domain. Scripture quotations marked AMP are taken from the Amplified® Bible (AMP). Copyright © 2015 by The Lockman Foundation. Used by permission. www.Lockman.org. Scripture quotations marked NASB95 are taken from the New American Standard Bible®. Copyright © 1960, 1971, 1977, 1995 by The Lockman Foundation. All rights reserved.

Stock or custom editions of BroadStreet Publishing titles may be purchased in bulk for educational, business, ministry, fundraising, or sales promotional use. For information, please email orders@broadstreetpublishing.com.

Design and typesetting | garborgdesign.com

Printed in China

21 22 23 24 25 5 4 3 2 1

ENDORSEMENTS

Now more than ever, fear is relentless; it never stops. The fear of death is a continual assault on our peace of mind. Like a storm, it can be all-consuming and unending, beating us down, eroding our sanity, stripping us of joy. This book has the cure.

Kirk Cameron
TV and Film Actor and Producer

Confession: When I was a child, the fear of death ruled my life. Even though I didn't have a clue who God was, I prayed obsessively that God would let me live forever. When I say obsessively, I mean fifty to a hundred times a day. If someone had given me Ray's latest book when I was a child, it would have saved me years of deathly terror. I know it will do the same for you.

Todd Friel
Host, *Wretched Radio/TV*

We are all fearful of the unknown. Especially when the subject is what happens to us when we die. My friend Ray Comfort will tell you how to overcome that fear, right here in this book. Read it now!

Tim Wildmon
President, American Family Association
and American Family Radio

The Bible reminds us that each one of us has an appointment with death. It is part of the human condition. Yet the thought of death can paralyze us with overwhelming fear. That is, unless you know that death doesn't get the last word and the awful sting of the grave has been removed. Because of what Christ did for us on the cross, paying the penalty for all our sins that brought death into the world, I was able to look at the lifeless body of my firstborn son and realize that I *will* see him again and be with him for all of eternity. I know that because he and I freely received what Jesus did for us at Calvary. Read Ray's book and discover that Christ has offered us everlasting life and the best is surely yet to come.

Janet Parshall
Host/Executive Producer, *In the Market with Janet Parshall*

Have you ever considered Jesus as a parachute or a lifeboat to save us from certain death? In this book, Ray Comfort employs these analogies to illustrate how we need not fear death. See how you can become a lighthouse for Jesus in this dark and stormy world!

Josh D. McDowell
Author

Perhaps you're thinking: *If there is a God, I'll get into heaven on my own steam. After all, I'm a pretty good person. My good deeds outweigh my bad. Therefore, I don't need Jesus to forgive my sins.* If you think that way, you've never met my brilliant friend Ray Comfort. In a minute or two, with just a couple of questions, Ray helps people realize that claim is not only unbiblical, but it wouldn't even hold up in a court of law. And Christianity is not just fire insurance for eternity. By trusting in Christ, you will also participate in the adventure you were made for in this life right now—to know God through Jesus Christ and to make him known to others (John 17:3, Matthew 28:19). Now let Ray take away your fear of death and show you how to live this exciting adventure right into eternity. It will be real life and anything but ordinary.

Frank Turek
Apologist, Author, Public Speaker, Radio Host
CrossExamined.org

DEDICATION

This book is dedicated to those who are still on this side of eternity, in the earnest hope that they will take seriously the Bible's amazing statement that Jesus Christ "has abolished death and brought life and immortality to light through the gospel" (see 2 Timothy 1:10).

TABLE OF CONTENTS

Foreword by John MacArthur   8

Preface   12

Chapter One: The Ultimate Intrusion   14

Chapter Two: Surely Genesis Is a Myth   23

Chapter Three: The Bible and the Scientific Method   36

Chapter Four: The Heart of the Issue   44

Chapter Five: A Rich Man's Big Mistake   54

Chapter Six: Solomon's Conclusion   69

Chapter Seven: When God Doesn't Answer   90

Chapter Eight: The Fight for Faith   109

Chapter Nine: Do Not Marvel   126

Chapter Ten: The Bedfellows   136

Chapter Eleven: A Lighthouse   153

Chapter Twelve: The Amazing Power of Conflict   159

Chapter Thirteen: The Evolution of Jerks   168

Chapter Fourteen: The Battle of Discouragement   177

More Promises about Fear   187

About the Author   191

FOREWORD

The COVID pandemic in 2020 exposed something significant about the effects of secularization on our society. It became clear that as our culture moves steadily farther away
from God, people are more burdened than ever with fear.
Most of all, they dread the end of this life, and they shrink
from any thought of what comes after. In the wake of the
coronavirus, fear of death spread like a plague though our
culture faster—and with more devastating results—than the
virus itself.

It is of course quite natural for fallen humanity to fear
death. Death is "the wages of sin" (Romans 6:23[1]), and it is
our most powerful and persistent enemy. Scripture says that
when Christ's triumph over every last vestige of evil is fully
realized, "the last enemy that will be abolished is death" (1
Corinthians 15:26).

Benjamin Franklin famously wrote, "In this world
nothing can be said to be certain, except death and taxes."
The truth is, there are many ways to avoid taxes. But there
is no way to avoid death. "In Adam *all* die" (1 Corinthians

---

1   All verses in this foreword are from the New American Standard Bible
1995 (NASB95).

15:22, emphasis added). "It is appointed for men to die once and after this comes judgment" (Hebrews 9:27). In other words, each of us has an appointment with the undertaker and a court date with the judge of the universe—and nothing in your future is any more certain than that.

Fear is the appropriate response for anyone who is unprepared for that reality. Not fear of death *per se,* but every soul should tremble at the thought of divine judgment. Jesus said, "Do not fear those who kill the body but are unable to kill the soul; but rather fear Him who is able to destroy both soul and body in hell" (Matthew 10:28). He was saying God is the One whom we should fear. Indeed, "The fear of the LORD is the beginning of wisdom" (Psalm 111:10; Proverbs 9:10).

The gospel, however, announces that repentant sinners can find grace and forgiveness so that they can truly face death not with fear but with full assurance of eternal life. The apostle Paul shows how and why. By his own description, he was the *foremost* of sinners. He had lived the life of a staunch Pharisee—self-righteous, hypocritical, and openly cruel toward others. He had once led a zealous campaign to put Christians to death for their faith. But then he was arrested by the gospel. His heart and mind were transformed. He wrote, "I found mercy, so that in me as the foremost, Jesus Christ might demonstrate His perfect patience as an example for those who would believe in Him for eternal life" (1 Timothy 1:16). After his conversion, he devoted all his energies to proclaiming the gospel he once tried to silence.

Fully aware that his efforts to take the gospel to the gentile world would ultimately cost him his life, he wrote, "We are of good courage, I say, and *prefer* rather to be absent from the body and to be at home with the Lord" (2 Corinthians 5:8, emphasis added). "To live is Christ and to die is gain" (Philippians 1:21). Paul's epistles are full of that confidence, even though the threat of death constantly pursued him—he was "beaten times without number, often in danger of death" (2 Corinthians 11:23). "I die daily," he wrote in 1 Corinthians 15:31.

He was ultimately arrested and condemned to die for preaching that Christ, not Caesar, is Lord of all. As the date of his execution drew near, he wrote, "I have fought the good fight, I have finished the course, I have kept the faith; in the future there is laid up for me the crown of righteous-ness, which the Lord, the righteous Judge, will award to me on that day; and not only to me, but also to *all who have loved His appearing*" (2 Timothy 4:7–8, emphasis added).

Every well-grounded Christian can likewise face death without fear, and the apostle deliberately stressed that truth. This was the whole reason Christ entered this world and died as an atoning sacrifice: so "that through death He might render powerless him who had the power of death, that is, the devil, and might free those who through fear of death were subject to slavery all their lives" (Hebrews 2:14–15).

Slavery is the right word for it. There is no more oppressive bondage than fear of death. To be gloriously liberated from that fear is the birthright of every genuine believer in Christ. If you long to be free from the fear of death, this book will be a great help and encouragement to you. Ray Comfort unfolds in careful detail the biblical message showing how it is possible to live and die with courage and secure confidence. This is a timely, edifying, crystal-clear study of how and why Christ is the answer to that oppressive burden of fear that is so often stirred by the thought of death. If you're looking for answers to the most daunting questions about life and death, time and eternity, this book is a perfect starting point.

May you be encouraged, may your faith be emboldened as you read, and may you know the peace of God that surpasses all human comprehension.

John MacArthur

PREFACE

Something frightening happened the very day I began to write this book. I had had writer's block for an entire week. It was so serious I thought that perhaps my writing days were over. That experience was unusual for me, but fortunately, the familiar flow had suddenly begun, and thoughts were jostling their way to the front of my mind like runners pushing against each other for the lead in the final lap of an Olympic race.

I was deep in thought as I rode my electric bike into a strong headwind—thankful for the effortless speed that kept me a little under twenty miles per hour. I leaned forward and said to my dog, as the wind blew back his white fur, "Is that good, Sam?" He loves standing on the platform I had made for him and was so intensely looking for cats and those of his own kind that he hardly acknowledged my question.

I had already glanced behind me. Nothing coming. In seconds we would be at our ministry building. I had planned to call Sue, my wife, when I entered the parking lot and tell her that I wouldn't be coming in. It was near dinnertime, so I would turn around and go straight home. That thought jostled in front of all the other runners. *Ah, the alleyway. I will turn now, and as I do, I will glance behind me to make sure that nothing is com—*

That very second, I heard a most frightening sound as I was about to turn. It was the roar of a large black SUV that must have pulled out from a parking space on the side of the road before accelerating past me. The driver had no idea I was about to suddenly turn left. As he roared past, he didn't know that I had escaped death by the skin of my teeth. If I hadn't heard that sudden roar, both myself and my precious dog would certainly have died. I had just had a near-death experience.

That night, after dinner, I soberly told Sue that she had come very close to being a widow that afternoon. My voice trembled, and tears welled in my widened eyes as I spoke.

I have thought over and over that had I turned one millisecond sooner, I would be in eternity...and you wouldn't be reading this book. But the grim reaper didn't take me, and now you're reading it. Perhaps I was divinely preserved for this very moment because God had you in mind that day.

Such a thought gives me great joy.

Best wishes,

Ray Comfort

May 2020

CHAPTER ONE

THE ULTIMATE INTRUSION

There are two things in life I hate with a passion. The first is disease-ridden, blood-sucking mosquitoes. Millions throughout the world know the misery of tiny welts that quickly erupt into a volcano of hot, itching lava for two or three miserable days. Sprays, scratching, ointments, ice, pills, and medications are mere temporary fixes. But one happy day my daughter told me that if I turn on a hair dryer on high and aim the heat at the welt for two minutes, the volcano will become extinct—the itching will stop.
I tried it, and to my surprise and delight, it worked! The key was to have it on as hot as I could stand it. That simple knowledge could take away days of misery for millions—if they only knew.

And that brings us to my second passionate hatred. The big one. Death. Knowledge can also save us from the power of death and the haunting fear that comes with it. Yet millions don't know: "My people are destroyed for lack of knowledge" (Hosea 4:6).

The Bible tells us the cause of death, it outlines precisely what happens after we die, and it gives us the wonderful cure—calling it "his unspeakable gift" (2 Corinthians 9:15 KJV). For the millions who believe God's Word, death is no mystery—and the cure that God has provided is a source of unspeakable comfort.

But the ungodly do not put any value on the gospel. Others mock it, and some even disdain the hope it offers. They remain willfully ignorant of the truth and "suppress the truth in unrighteousness" (Romans 1:18). They are tragically left with no light on the most important of issues— how to hold on to their most precious possession: their life.

The rejection of divine truth means that they are in darkness as to their origins, their true God-given purpose for existence, and their destiny when they pass into eternity. They don't know where they came from, what they're doing here, or where they're going after they die.

Alex Haley, the author of *Roots*, lamented:

> In all of us there is a hunger, marrow-deep, to know our heritage—to know who we are and where we have come from. Without this enriching knowledge, there is a hollow yearning. No matter what our

attainments in life, there is still a vacuum, an empti-
ness, and the most disquieting loneliness.[2]

But through the gospel, we know the truth, and the
truth frees us from futility, darkness, and despair. Until we
have that knowledge, we are truly lost, and Jesus said that
"the Son of Man [came] to seek and to save that which was
lost" (Luke 19:10). If you realize that you are lost today,
there is great hope that you can be found. Reading this
book is hopefully part of the journey to give you that precious knowledge, and after you possess it, may you whisper
with the writer of "Amazing Grace," *I once was lost, but now
I'm found.*

Nebulous Convictions

Ask most people about their beliefs on the subject of the
afterlife and you will find that they have built their convictions on other people's opinions, assumptions, or their own
hopes and personal feelings rather than on the solidity of
Scripture. Yet we shouldn't dismiss these often nebulous
convictions because God has placed eternity on our hearts
(see Ecclesiastes 3:11). We intuitively possess the echo of
Eden. Consequently, it's common to hear people say things
like, "There *must* be more..."

---

2   Alex Haley, "Quotable Quote," Goodreads, accessed on September 20,
2020, https://www.goodreads.com/quotes/25682-in-all-of-us-there-is-a-
hunger-marrow-deep-to.

Death is the ultimate intrusion. It is a massive and ugly elephant lifting its big and heavy foot and placing it upon any of us any time it wishes. God willing, of course. Nothing happens without his permission. This great beast casts its shadow over every human being. But it doesn't stop there. It enshrouds its darkness over the whole of life—over the beautiful rose, the cute little puppy, the tall and magnificent tree, and the bright-eyed and innocent child. The rose will wither, the puppy will grow old and die, so will the tall tree, and so will that bright-eyed and innocent child.

If you ask most people why death exists, they will shrug their shoulders and tell you that it's just the way it is. I know because I have asked thousands if they think there's an afterlife. They usually say that death is the *end* of life. It's natural. Everyone and everything dies. It's inevitable. Continue to press them as to *why* it's the end, and they draw a blank. To them, death just *is*, and we have to deal with it. Caesar, in Shakespeare's *Julius Caesar*, lambasts those as cowards who consider their end because he wrongly concludes that it is a natural and, therefore, a necessary end:

> Cowards die many times before their deaths.
> The valiant never taste of death but once.
> Of all the wonders that I yet have heard,
> It seems to me most strange that men should fear,
> Seeing that death, a necessary end,
> Will come when it will come.
> (William Shakespeare, *Julius Caesar*, Act 2, Scene 2)

Death isn't necessary because it is natural or hopelessly inevitable. It's necessary because of the law that demands "The soul who sins shall die" (Ezekiel 18:4).

Another question that draws an even bigger blank is why God gave us death in the first place. He's the maker of the beautiful rose. He gave it its brilliant color, its shapely and neatly layered petals, its magnificent fragrance, and its amazing ability to grow from a seed and to blossom. He also gave it the ability to reproduce more seed to produce more roses that continue to give us delight. Think of how many love-struck men (for a want of fitting words) have expressed their love for a woman with a rose. Think of how many flattered women have had their hearts melt as they take it in hand and admire its breathtaking beauty.

Yet, in a matter of days, that magnificent rose loses its wonderful fragrance, and its beautiful petals begin to drop like tears, one by one, to the ground. What remains of the gorgeous rose then turns brown, withers, and dies.

Everything withers and dies, including the gorgeous Hollywood actress. Her petals fall. Her attractive fragrance leaves, and she is cast aside by her industry as if she were worthless.

Even that magnificent hundred-year-old tall and strong tree will eventually follow in the sorrowful path of the withered rose. It's as though God has gifted us all these beautiful things, and then the cruelty of aging takes its hold until the icy-cold hand of death pulls them from our grasp. Why?

Uncontrollable tears once rolled down my cheeks like a river of unspeakable frustration because I didn't have an answer to that question: *Why?* It was early in the evening, back in September of 1971. I was a healthy twenty-one-year-old, happily married to a beautiful woman—with everything in life I could ever desire. And yet this question loomed over me like a haunting shadow and brought me to tears. *Why? Why did everything* have *to die?* It was a tragedy that didn't make sense. Little did I know that six months later I would come to understand the gospel, and it would shine a beam of glorious light into my frightening darkness. God hasn't left us in the shadow of death:

> The people who sat in darkness
> have seen a great light,
> And upon those who sat in the region
> and shadow of death
> Light has dawned. (Matthew 4:16)

THE NAIL IN OUR FOREHEAD

For many, the *why* of death is something that they do not let their minds fully consider. This approach reminds me of an interesting online video that cleverly helps men to understand the mysterious minds of women. Most men don't know that, commonly, a woman doesn't think like a man. To his manly mind it doesn't make any sense that a woman would deal with problems by talking them out. A problem to him isn't for him to talk about. It's for him to solve. He withdraws into a cave, thinks about it, and then comes out with a solution. But for many women, a burden shared is truly a burden halved.

This particular video shows a woman with a large nail sticking out of her forehead, telling her male friend that she has a terrible and mysterious headache. She doesn't know *why* her head hurts. Every time he tries to point to the nail, she becomes impatient and says that he really doesn't want to listen to her problems. All he cares about is his solution.

If you haven't already dealt with the nail in your forehead when it comes to death, I want to point it out, talk about it in depth, and then help you to pull it out—if you will let me.

While many in the world say that death is a natural part of life and that we have to accept it, the Bible tells a different story. Death isn't the cessation of life. It's an appointment we have to keep: "And as it is appointed for men to die once, but after this the judgment" (Hebrews 9:27).

Much like earthly judicial courts that issue subpoenas, or summonses to appear, for legal cases, the Lord has issued us a divine subpoena. In other words, we must appear before God to face judgment. If we choose not to appear, we're in big trouble.

And in reality, the divine subpoena leaves us without *any* choice. Death is coming, ready or not, as the arresting officer. The grim reaper is going to make sure we appear before the judge of the universe to stand trial for our many transgressions. Such thoughts are very unnerving for the guilty. But don't draw back from the light. Stay with me. We need to talk this out.

Let's ask why we are in this fateful position. The Bible says that the problem of death originated way back in the garden of Eden: "Therefore, just as through one man sin entered the world, and death through sin, and thus death spread to all men, because all sinned" (Romans 5:12).

Adam is solely to blame for ushering in death. That seems grossly unfair to his descendants. We didn't ask to be born, and yet here we are—waiting to die because of one man's original transgression. Some would surmise that it would have been better not to have been born. We were condemned to death from the moment we came into this life.

We learned about Adam's role in bringing death to humanity from the first book of the Bible. In the next chapter we are going to ask if the book of Genesis has any serious credibility. Can it be relied upon, or is it just one example of mythology that previous generations have passed down to us?

WORDS OF COMFORT

Fear not, for I am with you;
Be not dismayed, for I am your God.
I will strengthen you,
Yes, I will help you,
I will uphold you with My righteous right hand.
(Isaiah 41:10)

It's been said that the words *fear not* appear 366 times in the Bible—one for every day of the year and one for the leap year. Every day can bring with it different fears, but trust in God is like an umbrella that protects us when the thunderstorm sends rain. As long as we have faith in his exceedingly great and precious promises, we will be sheltered from tormenting fear.

If we are trusting in Jesus, God is no longer against us. He is both with us and for us. When we are weak, he will strengthen us; when we are helpless, he will help us; and when we fall, he will uphold us with his ready and steady righteous right hand.

CHAPTER TWO

SURELY GENESIS IS A MYTH

The book of Genesis gives us an explanation for the origin of death. It came through Adam and spread like a deadly plague upon all of his descendants.

Many believe that science has disapproved that the God of the Old Testament created the world in six days. Additionally, most of this generation believe that Darwinian evolution is a *proven* scientific fact. Period. The evidence is in. In the minds of many people, there's no argument.

And what does Darwin say about death? According to evolutionary theory:

> As life goes on, your genes effectively stop caring what happens to you. After a certain point, it's so unlikely that you're still alive that your genes can safely assume you'll already be dead. So your

genomic programming can contain all sorts of wacky stuff that only kicks in after this point, just because there's no noticeable selection against it.

The really fascinating part (by which I mean the really depressing part) is how this effect reinforces itself. The more likely it is that you're dead, the less your genes care about you. The less your genes care about you, the more likely it is that you're dead. This has been going on throughout our evolutionary history, so we've accumulated all sorts of weird malfunctions that kick in late in our lives. The human genome is riddled with them, and most of the genes involved are also part of normal development and reproduction. These malfunctions cluster around a certain age: the age when evolution stops caring about us because, statistically speaking, we're already dead.

So mortality is an evolutionary prophecy that fulfills itself in a multitude of ways. And that's why there's no single key to eternal life.[3]

This surety of your own genes abandoning you once you're no longer an asset to evolution is not a happy thought. But evolutionists view this process—view

---

3   Suzanne Sadedin, "Biologically Speaking, This Is Why Humans Are Born To Die," *Forbes*, July 13, 2016, https://www.forbes.com/sites/quora/2016/07/13/biologically-speaking-this-is-why-humans-are-born-to-die/?sh=39af63f44a48.

death—as natural, ordinary, everyday. It may not be happy, but it's the way things are supposed to be.

So which is true? Did human beings evolve by chance over time, or did God miraculously create mankind as male and female? Is death a divine curse, or is it a natural occurrence, just a step in the process of evolution?

Evolutionary biologists sometimes speak with an almost divine authority: "And that's why there's no single key to eternal life." However, it's wise not to take everything they say as gospel. How do we, therefore, know which one we should trust—evolution theory or creationism?

To answer this important question, we will apply the scientific method to both evolution and creationism. The dictionary defines *the scientific method* as "principles and procedures for the systematic pursuit of knowledge involving the recognition and formulation of a problem, the collection of data through observation and experiment, and the formulation and testing of hypotheses."[4]

Essentially, the scientific method says that something must be both observable and testable to be credible.

First, we will look for a few moments at Darwinian evolution—the argument that man and primates have a common ancestor. Unfortunately for its advocates, evolution doesn't pass the scientific method—because it can't. It's

---

4   "Scientific method." *Merriam-Webster.com Dictionary*, Merriam-Webster, accessed on February 9, 2021, https://www.merriam-webster.com/dictionary/scientific%20method.

impossible to observe or test Darwinian evolution because it supposedly happened sixty-three million years ago:

> 63 million years ago: The primates split into two groups, known as the haplorrhines (dry-nosed primates) and the strepsirrhines (wet-nosed primates). The strepsirrhines eventually become the modern lemurs and aye-ayes, while the haplorrhines develop into monkeys and apes—and humans.[5]

Therefore, everything believed about the theory must be received in blind faith. As a result, evolution believers have their own evolutionary language when presenting a belief. They will say things like "probably," "maybe," "perhaps," or "could have." Nothing is concrete in evolutionary thought because it cannot pass the scientific method. It's not *scientifically* credible. It's unproven and unprovable.

MALE AND FEMALE

These days, many female supporters of Darwinism seem to have overlooked that when it comes to Darwinian evolution, women don't exist. The evolutionary charts that show the process of small, bent-over apes slowly evolving into modern man are males. Women never feature because it would obviously provoke the question as to why a female

---

5   Michael Marshall, "Timeline: The evolution of life," *NewScientist*, July 14, 2009, https://www.newscientist.com/article/dn17453-timeline-the-evolution-of-life/.

would suddenly appear. If they *did* decide to include women in evolutionary history, do they have the female bending beside the first male primate, the second, third, or fourth?

Scientists don't have a clue as to why women would evolve in the evolutionary process—because there was no obvious advantage, something that believers believe must be present for evolution to take place. The process of evolution supposedly happens slowly over time as natural selection causes those with helpful mutations/developments to survive and thus reproduce and pass their traits. However, "Evolutionists freely admit that the origin of the sexual process remains one of the most difficult problems in biology."[6] Further evidence shows,

> Evolutionists have practically been forced to concede that there must be "some advantage" to a system as physiologically and energetically complex as sex—as Mark Ridley admitted when he wrote: "It is highly likely that sex has some advantage, and that the advantage is big. Sex would not have evolved, and been retained, unless it had some advantage." Yet finding and explaining that advantage seems to have eluded our evolutionary colleagues. Sir John Maddox, who served for over twenty-five years as the distinguished editor of *Nature*, the prestigious journal published by the British Association for the Advancement

---

6   J.F. Crow, *The Importance of Recombination, The Evolution of Sex: An Examination of Current Ideas*, (Sunderland, MA: Sinauer Associates, 1988), 35.

of Science (and who was knighted by Queen Elizabeth II in 1994 for "multiple contributions to science"), authored an amazing book titled *What Remains to be Discovered* in which he addressed the topic of the origin of sex, and stated forthrightly:

"The overriding question is when (and then how) sexual reproduction itself evolved. Despite decades of speculation, we do not know."[7]

In a process that depends on developing the most efficient and foolproof methods of survival, why would sexual reproduction, something that requires two separate organisms working together, evolve out of asexual reproduction? When, how, and why women evolved isn't known, and putting her into the evolutionary chart would open a can of unanswered and, it seems, unanswerable worms. Scientists have, however, come to some interesting conclusions as to why women are in the shape they are in:

We were brainstorming features that distinguish our species, *Homo sapiens*, from other primates. That list includes human peculiarities like big brains, upright walking, language, furless bodies...and permanently enlarged breasts after puberty.

In other primate species, only pregnant or lactating females have bosoms. The animals stay

---

7   Brad Harrub and Bert Thompson, "Evolutionary Theories on Gender and Sexual Reproduction," Creation.com (PDF), TJ 18(1) 2004, 98.

flat-chested for the rest of their lives. In humans, pubescent girls accumulate fat around their milk glands, which stays for life and seems to hold sex appeal in every culture. Those permanent, alluring mounds of fat on women's chests are indeed an evolutionary anomaly, begging for an explanation.

Over the years, researchers have proposed a number of explanations for human breasts. Some claimed evolution favored "pendulous" breasts—as scientists dryly describe them—because they gave babies something to cling to like handle bars. Others suggested permanent breasts evolved as an energy reserve, lumps of fat to be tapped when food is scarce. From this perspective, women's breasts may have originally functioned liked camel's humps.[8]

There you have it, ladies. God didn't make you as you are. You're an accident that in time became a meaningless primate whose unique features possibly evolved for the same reason a bike has handlebars and a camel has humps.

Charles Darwin not only believed that women were hairy primates, but he believed that they were inferior:

In *The Descent of Man*, Darwin argued that evolution made man "superior" to woman. For Darwin, that

---

8   Bridget Alex, "Scientists Still Stumped By the Evolution of Human Breasts," *Discover* Magazine (website), March 6, 2019, https://www. discovermagazine.com/planet-earth/scientists-still-stumped-by-the-evolution-of-human-breasts.

superiority largely played out in the intellectual and artistic realm. He wrote: "If two lists were made of the most eminent men and women in poetry, painting, sculpture, music—comprising composition and performance, history science and philosophy...the two lists would not bear comparison." [Social scientist Herbert] Spencer echoed Darwin's sentiments and went further, postulating that in order for the human race to flourish, women must devote their lives to reproduction.[9]

The book of Genesis, however, gives a woman great honor and tremendous worth. She is not inferior. Instead, like Adam, she has been made in God's image—as a helpmate who was to be treated with love and tenderness. And God made her as he had made Adam, naked: "And they were both naked, the man and his wife, and were not ashamed" (Genesis 2:25).

Scripture uses the word *wife*. It is the *marriage* bed that is undefiled (see Hebrews 13:4). Look now at what the Bible says about her "handlebars"—her shapely form and how the man should respond:

> Let your fountain be blessed,
> And rejoice with the wife of your youth.
> As a loving deer and a graceful doe,

9   Rebekkah Rubin, "The Woman Who Challenged Darwin's Sexism," *Smithsonian* Magazine (website), November 9, 2017, https://www.smithsonianmag.com/science-nature/woman-who-tried-take-down-darwin-180967146/.

Let her breasts satisfy you at all times;
And always be enraptured with her love.
(Proverbs 5:18–19)

Again, Scripture uses the qualifying word: *wife*.

God not only created Adam and Eve naked, with a fully formed reproductive ability, he told them to have sex (see Genesis 1:28). In the biblical account of creation, sex is logical and central to the picture from the very start. Having two genders is not an unexplainable phenomenon that suddenly happened sometime in our history but an intrinsic aspect of our species from the very start.

CHANCE

We've discussed how human reproduction makes little sense in the evolutionary theory. But even beyond that, everything else that pertains to the miracle of life, according to evolution, was because of luck. It was fairytale magic that it came together. Read how NASA likened what happened to a fairytale:

> Researchers are finding that life can thrive in some unexpected places.
> "This porridge is too hot," Goldilocks exclaimed.
> So she tasted the porridge from the second bowl.
> "This porridge is too cold."
> So she tasted the last bowl of porridge.
> "Ahhh, this porridge is just right!" she said happily.

And she ate it all up.

"Goldilocks and the 3 Bears" children's story

For many years they looked around the solar system. Mercury and Venus were too hot. Mars and the outer planets were too cold. Only Earth was just right for life, they thought. Our planet has liquid water, a breathable atmosphere, a suitable amount of sunshine. Perfect.

It didn't have to be that way. If Earth were a little closer to the sun it might be like hot choking Venus; a little farther, like cold arid Mars. Somehow, though, we ended up in just the right place with just the right ingredients for life to flourish. Researchers of the 1970s scratched their heads and said we were in "the Goldilocks Zone."[10]

Add to the insanity the thought that most who trust in evolution tend toward atheism. They think that there was no need for a Creator. They believe the scientific impossibility that nothing created everything. They don't believe that everything came from nothing. They believe that nothing was the initial cause. But nothing could be further from the truth. Nothing can't create anything because it's nothing. Nothing *is* nothing, *says* nothing, and *does* nothing because it's nothing and, therefore, can't create anything. It couldn't possibly happen—not in a million years.

---

10 "The Goldilocks Zone," NASA Science (website), October 2, 2003, https://science.nasa.gov/science-news/science-at-nasa/2003/02oct_goldilocks.

Think of the folly of believing that a rose made itself. Think of nothing exploding and, through the fairy godmother of time, making a puppy (male or female), a kitten (male or female), the predictably precise timing of the daily sunrise, the reliability of the yearly seasons, all the fruits, night and day, conscious thought, morality, and human beings as male and female. The story of Cinderella's pumpkin turning into a coach has much more credibility—because it includes an initial cause.

Evolution's Explanation

Evolution is hopeless and helpless in the face of death. It just is. In an article entitled, "A Problem for Darwin: Why Do We Age and Die Rather Than Live Forever?" published in *Psychology Today*, Dr. Ira Rosofsky said,

> Yet aging presents an apparent paradox for evolutionary theory. The basic premise of evolution—natural selection—is that some randomly appearing traits are better fitted for survival than others. Individuals with those preferential traits will survive to pass them on to new generations. Among humans, mental acuity—the ability to plan the hunting and gathering—and physical prowess—the ability to execute the hunting and gathering are two of the human traits that with great success survived and evolved.

But with aging comes dementia and frailty. Where's the advantage in that?

Dr. Rosofsky went on to quote Leonid A. Gavrilov and Natalia S. Gavrilova:

> "How does it happen that, after having accomplished the miraculous success that led us from a single cell at conception through birth and then to sexual maturity and productive adulthood...the developmental program formed by biological evolution fails even to maintain the accomplishments of its own work?"

Rosofsky then said,

> The co-discover[er] of natural selection, Alfred [Russel] Wallace, hypothesized "programmed death" as an explanation for aging, "...when one or more individuals have provided a sufficient number of successors they themselves, as consumers of nourishment in a constantly increasing degree, are an injury to those successors. Natural selection therefore weeds them out."[11]

Evolution thinks the elderly are nothing of worth—just useless weeds.

---

11   Ira Rosofsky, "A Problem for Darwin: Why Do We Age And Die Rather Than Live Forever?," Psychology Today (website), March 7, 2009, https://www.psychologytoday.com/us/blog/adventures-in-old-age/200903/problem-darwin-why-do-we-age-and-die-rather-live-forever.

WORDS OF COMFORT

> Be anxious for nothing, but in everything by prayer and supplication, with thanksgiving, let your requests be made known to God; and the peace of God, which surpasses all understanding, will guard your hearts and minds through Christ Jesus. (Philippians 4:6–7)

To be *anxious* means to be experiencing worry, unease, or nervousness, typically about an imminent event or something with an uncertain outcome. The way to rid yourself of that fear is to commit the outcome (whatever it may be) to God through prayer. Show that you trust God by adding the mix of "thanksgiving," and the fruit of your trust will be the peace of God guarding your heart and mind. It is to say, *Dear Father, I don't understand what's going on, but I put my hand in yours and trust you that all will be well because you are faithful.*

CHAPTER THREE

THE BIBLE AND THE SCIENTIFIC METHOD

Perhaps you are feeling that you have been forced into a conundrum. The Bible is offering you a very real hope in life and in your death, but the world says that it is unscientific and shouldn't be taken seriously. But don't believe the unbelievers because the Bible stands as a rock in the face of scientific inquiry. Those who would laugh at such a statement have almost certainly never humbly studied the pages of the world's biggest selling book. I have poured over it diligently, and that's why I wrote a best-selling book called *Scientific Facts in the Bible: 100 Reasons to Believe the Bible Is Supernatural in Origin.*

We can look at a few examples here of the Bible's trustworthiness. Look at this wonderful irony regarding the opening words of Genesis:

> For over a century, scientists have recognized that all natural phenomena in the Universe can ultimately be divided into interactions between five basic, fundamental "manifestations." In 1882, staunch evolutionist Herbert Spencer, an English philosopher, biologist, and sociologist who was a prominent classical liberal political theorist of the Victorian era, recognized "likenesses and unlikenesses among phenomena,…which are segregated into manifestations, …and then into space and time, matter and motion and force…" (Soylent Communications, 2011, emp. added). In *First Principles*, under the chapter heading, "Space, Time, Matter, Motion, and Force," he wrote, "These modes of cohesion under which manifestations are invariably presented, and therefore invariably represented, we call…Space and Time,… Matter and Motion [action—JM]" (1882, 1:171, emp. added). "Though Space, Time, Matter, and Motion, are apparently all necessary data of intelligence, yet a psychological analysis…shows us that these are either built up of, or abstracted from, experiences of Force" (p. 169). So, time, force, action, space, and matter are the five manifestations of all scientific phenomena.

This truth—fundamental to understanding science—was articulated by an agnostic in the 19th century, and yet these fundamental principles were articulated in the very first verse of the Bible millennia ago. "In the beginning [time], God [force] created [action] the heavens [space] and the Earth [matter]." It is truly amazing that a renowned apostle of agnosticism would be the one to verbally articulate this discovery from science—a discovery which gives significant weight to the contention that one can know there is a God and that the Bible is His inspired Word. And further, it is notably ironic that the very man from whom Charles Darwin took the phrase, "survival of the fittest" (Spencer, 1864, 2:444), would be the man that unknowingly found evidence specifically supporting the inspiration of Genesis chapter one—the very chapter of the Bible that relates the truth about man's origin. Acts 14:17 rightly says, "Nevertheless He did not leave Himself without witness, in that He did good."[12]

If you fell into the ocean and you couldn't swim, you may think you have good reason to panic. However, if, instead of being gripped by terror, you experimentally extended your legs and found yourself standing on a rock

12   Jeff Miller, "The Five Manifestations of Natural Phenomena," Apologetics Press, accessed on September 15, 2020, http://apologeticspress.org/APContent.aspx?category=13&article=751.

shelf a few feet beneath the surface, the knowledge that
the rock is able to support your weight would immediately
relieve you of your fears. Then again, you could lift your feet
off the rock, worrying if it could support your weight, or you
could rest on it until you are rescued. The choice is yours.

Scripture is a solid rock. Jesus said that it cannot be
broken (see John 10:35). You *can* trust it. You don't need
to feel intellectually inferior for believing in the Bible and
having faith. If you are feeling alone, take a few moments
to look up and study a long list of the many believers
who are or have been involved in the fields of science and
technology. Consider Galileo, a brilliant Italian often called
the "father of the scientific method," who was extremely
successful in physics, engineering, and astronomy. Or think
of Francis Bacon, whose insightful "works argued for the
possibility of scientific knowledge based only upon induc-
tive reasoning and careful observation of events in nature."[13]

Also, a little thought can help when reading Genesis.
Its words can be observed and tested by everyday life.
Approximately one hundred fifty thousand human beings
die every day throughout the world—that's a massive
fifty-four million every year! And every one is a cold and
stark reality that confirms the truth of Scripture. Every one
of the useless cursed billions upon billions of weeds that
push through the earth stands as a testimony to the truth

---

13   "Frances Bacon," Wikipedia, accessed February 9, 2021, https://
en.wikipedia.org/wiki/Francis_Bacon.

of Genesis. So does every drop of sweat and every pain in childbirth. The accuracy of the Genesis fall is seen in the ground-shaking reality of earthquakes, massive floods, devastating droughts, horrific hurricanes, terrorizing tornadoes, terrible tsunamis, deadly diseases, and, of course, endless human pain and suffering.

The explanation for all these painful thorns given to us in the book of Genesis can be observed and tested. It passes the scientific method. It also gives us the origin of evil. Evil entered the human race through Adam. To observe its reality, we merely need to look at the onslaught of daily news. It is like a dam bursting with rape, murder, racism, theft, lying, adultery, fornication, homosexuality, pornography, blasphemy, greed, anger, hatred, and the spinoffs of endless corruption.

Genesis also gives us the origin of light, of the breathtakingly beautiful skies, and of this wonderful earth—of the thousands of amazing fish, birds, and other animals. The Scriptures say that when God had made them, that they were "finished." Adam wasn't made with evolving eyes that wouldn't work until all the needed parts had developed. How could a semi-evolved heart pump semi-evolved blood through half-evolved blood vessels? How could Adam swallow without a fully evolved epiglottis? How did he breathe before his lungs evolved? None of his vital organs could keep him alive unless they were complete—"finished," as the Bible says. This is just common sense. It's also the First Law of Thermodynamics:

> The Hebrew word for completed is kalah (כָּלָה, Strong's 3615). It means "completed, finished, at an end." The use of the past definite tense for the Hebrew verb indicates action completed in the past, never to occur again. Creation was finished and done. Matter and energy are no longer being created.[14]

Evolution is scientifically impossible. And yet, some theists try and squeeze evolution into Scripture, but it doesn't fit. They dismiss a literal Genesis and say that God used evolution when he created everything. But that thought is blown out of the face of the waters by one verse of Scripture. Jesus said, "Have you not read that He who made them at the beginning 'made them male and female?'" (Matthew 19:4).

God made them male and female. He didn't begin with a cell that then evolved by itself for millions of years until it became a primate, which, over time, branched into an upright walking and talking hairy human. He made male and female—fully furnished and finished—with a working brain, seeing eyes, chewing teeth, tasting tastebuds, a functioning stomach, a working liver, operational kidneys, breathing lungs, soft and sensitive skin, wonderful

---

14   "Science in the Bible–Thermodynamics," Bible-Science Guy, April 26, 2017, https://biblescienceguy.wordpress.com/2017/04/26/science-in-the-bible-thermodynamics/.

mechanical hands, life-giving blood, fully formed blood vessels to carry it to the body, complete with the ability to reproduce after their own kind.

The Reason for All This Reasoning

If Darwinism is true and scientifically believable, then what it says about death is true. But consider the conclusion: Death is totally out of your control. There is nothing you can do but wait for the grim reaper to cut you down. The theory offers you nothing but bad news because it's horribly bleak and brutal and hopeless.

However, if the Bible's account of creation is true and scientifically credible, which it clearly is, that means that what the Bible has to say about death is also true. So let's go look at what Scripture says on the subject in the next few chapters.

WORDS OF COMFORT

Whenever I am afraid, I will trust in You.
(Psalm 56:3)

"Whenever" rightly assumes that our battle against fear is ongoing. It begins in childhood and continues to try and haunt us in our old age. This is because the Bible speaks of "the spirit of fear" (see 2 Timothy 1:7). A soldier must ignore his fears and instead daily clothe himself with the armor of courage. When fear comes, he resists it by trusting in his *weapons*, the *cause* for which he fights, and the *hope* of final victory. He cannot lose sight of any of these. Neither can the soldier of Christ as he or she fights the good fight of faith. Our weapons of faith in Jesus and our love for God will not fail us as long as we remain steadfast in our hope of final victory—a hope that is "an anchor for the soul, both sure and steadfast" (Hebrews 6:19). Whenever I'm afraid, I *will* trust in you.

CHAPTER FOUR

THE HEART OF THE ISSUE

There is a local freeway that regularly gives me an adrenaline rush (and near cardiac arrest). As I drive up the on-ramp, I know that I only have a short distance to get across three lanes to the left. If I don't get across, I will be pushed in the wrong direction by the stampede of speeding vehicles that need to frantically cross into the *right* three lanes to avoid heading in the wrong direction themselves. This portion of the freeway was designed by a man whose brother-in-law was an undertaker.

I put my foot down and increase my speed from a modest thirty miles an hour to seventy miles an hour in a matter of seconds. The perceived speed differential between my vehicle and the other traffic is frighteningly evident. Massive trucks are on my left, a big SUV is racing toward me in my rearview mirror. I'm watching the maneuvering motorist in front of me, trying to increase my speed but at the same time keep a safe distance. As I jostle to get into the first lane (at what seems like 150 miles an hour), I am saying, *Please let me in. Does anyone care? This is my precious life! Somebody feel sorry for me!* The problem for me is that the speeding drivers see me as nothing but a dangerous hindrance to their frantic goal. If ever there were a need for the Golden Rule of treating others as you would have them treat you, it is when we are entering a fast-moving freeway and need to cross lanes.

Life is like a frightening freeway—where millions frantically jostle daily to avoid being taken out by death. Many live in a private panic. The fear of death and a sense of futility haunt them as each day dawns.

But there is a very real hope. The word *gospel* means good news, and that good news is that almighty God came down in the person of Jesus to save us from death. No words in the English language can begin to express how amazingly wonderful this is. Even the apostle Paul was at a loss for words. As we have seen earlier, he called what we have in the gospel, the "unspeakable gift" (2 Corinthians 9:15 KJV). In this chapter, we will look closer at why we so desperately need this gift.

WHEN FEAR IS YOUR FRIEND

During World War II, Adolf Hitler (after he ordered the attack of Russia) promised the German army that they would march through Moscow. And they certainly did. On July 17, 1944, a contingent of 57,000 German soldiers marched through the streets of Moscow—*as prisoners of war*. Approximately three million German prisoners of war were captured by the Soviet Union during World War II, most of them during the great advances of the Red Army in the last year of the war.

Most think that when we die, all is well with God and that we're going to march into heaven. But the Bible says otherwise...that we are instead being held captive to do the will of the devil:

> And a servant of the Lord must not quarrel but be gentle to all, able to teach patient, in humility correcting those who are in opposition, if God perhaps will grant them repentance, so that they may know the truth, and that they may come to their senses and escape the snare of the devil, *having been taken captive by him to do his will.* (2 Timothy 2:24–26, emphasis added)

We have this presumption because we are ignorant as to the serious nature of sin. But sin is so serious to God that he has put all humanity on death row, and the Bible says that we are then tormented by the fear of death through our entire lives:

> Therefore, since [these His] children share in flesh and blood [the physical nature of mankind], He Himself in a similar manner also shared in the same [physical nature, but without sin], so that through [experiencing] death He might make powerless (ineffective, impotent) him who had the power of death—that is, the devil—and [that He] might free all those who through [the haunting] fear of death were held in slavery throughout their lives. (Hebrews 2:14–15 AMP)

The world has tried to soften its reality by giving us alternative words when we speak of death. Instead of saying that someone died, we say that they passed on. We celebrate their life. They didn't get buried in a graveyard. Rather, they rest in a memorial park. An undertaker becomes a funeral director, and the hearse becomes a limo. Despite the change in language, death is still horrific.

However, this dread we feel can be beneficial—because not all fear is bad. Sometimes it's there to protect us. It doesn't *feel* good, but it *is* good.

It doesn't feel good to stand on the edge of a thousand-foot cliff and experience terror when we look down. But that discomfort *is* good because the terror will make us step back from the cliff, *if we listen to it.* Therefore, listen to the God-given fear of death. It's saying, *Back up, back up. Get yourself out of danger!*

The tragedy is that most people feel the fear, and yet they don't move back from the cliff. They think that death is natural—that it's part of life or that there's nothing we can do about it. They believe it is inevitable.

But death is not natural. It's not your friend. The Bible says it's your enemy (see 1 Corinthians 15:26), and if we don't fear an enemy, we are not wise. We should fear death not just because death itself is fearful, but also because after death, we will move out of the frying pan into the fire. We have to face a holy God on the day of judgment. And that is a fearful thing. Jesus said to those who are his friends:

> And I say to you, My friends, do not be afraid of those who kill the body, and after that have no more that they can do. But I will show you whom you should fear: Fear Him who, after He has killed, has power to cast into hell; yes, I say to you, fear Him! (Luke 12:4–5)

Jesus was saying that someone who was rushing toward you with a knife to plunge it into your chest is not to be feared compared to the fear of standing before God in our sins: "It is a fearful thing to fall into the hands of the living God" (Hebrews 10:31).

When we speak of a guilty criminal *falling into the hands of the law*, the inference is that when we fall into something, we have no choice and no way of escape. And that's our predicament: "How shall we escape if we neglect so great a salvation?" (Hebrews 2:3).

THE DIFFERENCE A PARACHUTE MAKES

A good dentist may *hurt* you, but he will not *harm* you. He may cause you to have some pain, but he does his job because he wants to save your teeth. And you let him do that because you know the end result.

I'm now going to probe into areas that you may consider to be none of my business. I'm going to touch a raw nerve, but I do it because I don't want you to be harmed on judgment day. I believe you are in danger of losing your soul, and I want you to be saved. So please be patient with me as I pointedly probe.

Knowing that we have to die is like standing at the door of a plane ten thousand feet up and waiting to jump without a parachute. It is horrific. You know that you are going to fall for a long thirty to forty seconds at one hundred twenty miles per hour and hit the unforgiving ground on your face. Such thoughts take our breath away. Everything within us screams, *Noooooo!*

Here, now, is how to be free from the haunting fear of death:

Imagine, as you stand helpless and hopeless on the edge of the plane, some kind person gives you a parachute that you know was expertly packed by someone who loved you. You also recognize the label on it. It is a new type of parachute that has been tested more than one hundred thousand times, and it never fails to open. Ever. It is utterly fail proof.

As you put the parachute on, what is your attitude toward the jump now? How is it different? Now you *know* that you're not going to hit the ground at one hundred twenty miles per hour. Rather, you are going to land gently at twelve miles per hour on your feet. Your faith in the parachute has given you the ability to control your fears. You are no longer tormented by fear because you know that gravity has no power over you.

Listen closely because this is unarguably the most important thing you will ever hear:

Almighty God has provided a perfect parachute in the Savior. But you're not going to want to completely trust in him unless you realize you have to face a law that is far harsher than gravity. That's why I'm taking the time to talk about sin and the danger in which it leaves us.

Let's go back to the plane scenario before the parachute was offered. Imagine if there was someone who didn't listen to his fears and he instead was deluded into thinking that there wasn't any danger. He would not be interested in the offer of a parachute. If we don't tremble because we have sinned against God, we are like that person. The Bible says "The fear of the LORD is the beginning of wisdom" (Proverbs 9:10). So I am going to try to do you the greatest of favors. I'm going to love you enough to attempt to put the fear of God in you—and I will do it by looking at the law you must face after you die.

As we look at this law, you will hopefully become a little fearful. Unpleasant though it may be, it will be good for you. Again, think of why you would put on a parachute— it's because you will have to jump, and the fear makes you want to trust it. It gives you very *real* incentive. Fear, in that case, becomes your friend. It's very important to keep that in mind.

THOSE ANNOYING TYPOS

I know that I'm not alone when it comes to unwittingly putting typos in a phone text. We write our message, quickly proofread it, send it, and to our embarrassment, we reread it the next day and see a glaring typo.

I thought that I had written, "I'd like to buy you a cat." However, I actually wrote, "I'd like to buy you a car." The reason I didn't notice the obvious typo was because in my mind, I am imaging a cat, and that thought overrides the misspelling. It's when I have forgotten the text's context and therefore don't have a cat sitting in my imagination that I'm able to look at the text objectively and see my error.

In our fallen state we have a propensity to think we are right when we are wrong. We quickly pass over important matters, assuming that we know the truth without taking the time to consider it objectively. A typo in a text is just a typo in a text. It's no big deal. But we can't afford to be wrong when it comes to the way of salvation: "There is a way that seems right to a man, But its end is the way of death" (Proverbs 14:12). And, "He who trusts his own heart is a fool" (Proverbs 28:26).

In the next chapter, we will take the time to examine the truth, no matter how uncomfortable it is. We'll start discovering what the Bible has to say about what comes after death by looking at a very rich man who thought he had it right when it came to his beliefs about how to get to heaven. He didn't.

WORDS OF COMFORT

> I, even I, am He who comforts you.
> Who are you that you should be afraid
> Of a man who will die,
> And of the son of a man who will be made like grass?
> (Isaiah 51:12)

It's easy to miss the fact that it is almighty God himself who is speaking these words. He says that he is the one who comforts us. This is because he is the lover of our souls. His love for us isn't drawn out because we are lovable. But because God is love, and those who love and trust him don't fear man.

CHAPTER FIVE

A RICH MAN'S BIG MISTAKE

Scripture tells us that Jesus was approached by a young man who had "great possessions":

> Now as He was going out on the road, one came running, knelt before Him, and asked Him, "Good Teacher, what shall I do that I may inherit eternal life?" So Jesus said to him, "Why do you call Me good? No one is good but One, that is, God. You know the commandments: 'Do not commit adultery,' 'Do not murder,' 'Do not steal,' 'Do not bear false witness,' 'Do not defraud,' 'Honor your father and your mother.'" And he answered and said to Him, "Teacher, all these things I have kept from my youth." Then Jesus, looking at him, loved him, and said to him,

"One thing you lack: Go your way, sell whatever you have and give to the poor, and you will have treasure in heaven; and come, take up the cross, and follow Me." But he was sad at this word, and went away sorrowful, for he had great possessions. (Mark 10:17–22)

This story is also found in Matthew 19:16–23 and Luke 18:18–23. In Matthew 19:16 we are given more details: "Now behold, one came and said to him, 'Good Teacher, *what good thing* shall I do that I may have eternal life?'" (emphasis added).

His big mistake was to think that he had to do some "good thing" to obtain eternal life. This is the way that *seems* right to most of us, but that way ends in death. It is a mistake, and the way to see this glaring error is to look at it objectively.

Even though it may look to some that Jesus is saying that we can obtain everlasting life by selling whatever we have and giving it to the poor, that would mean that anyone could *purchase* everlasting life. It would mean that even a poor man who only owned one old donkey could sell it, give the proceeds to the poor and, in exchange, receive everlasting life. Whereas it would cost a multi-billionaire billions of dollars. Anyone who owned anything material could *buy* everlasting life from God, and that would fly in the face of many other verses that tell us that salvation cannot be purchased (Romans 3:20, 28; 4:6; Galatians 2:16; Ephesians 2:9; 2 Timothy 1:9):

> Those who trust in their wealth
> And boast in the multitude of their riches,
> None of them can by any means redeem his brother,
> Nor give to God a ransom for him—
> For the redemption of their souls is costly,
> And it shall cease forever—
> That he should continue to live eternally,
> And not see the Pit. (Psalm 49:6–9)

While Jesus was quoting the Commandments, he may have given us a subtle clue about *how* the rich young ruler obtained his wealth. He added "Do not defraud" in with five of the Ten Commandments (see Mark 10:19). It would seem that this man was rich because he had engaged in fraud—he had obtained his wealth by *illegal* means, and that's why Jesus told him to give his money to the poor (those from whom he had presumably stolen) and then to follow him.

It then looks as though Jesus was saying that the way of salvation is to obey the Ten Commandments. And that would be the case *if* we could obey them. Scripture actually promises that (see Luke 10:27–28). But if we transgress the moral law even in one point, we come under its wrath and receive the sentence of death:

> For whoever shall keep the whole law, and yet
> stumble in one point, he is guilty of all. For He who
> said, "Do not commit adultery," also said, "Do not

murder." Now if you do not commit adultery, but you do murder, you have become a transgressor of the law. (James 2:10–11)

HAVE YOU EARNED YOUR WAGES?

Death, according to the Bible, is *wages*. The Scriptures say, "The *wages* of sin is death" (Romans 6:23, emphasis added). As mentioned earlier, sin is so serious to God that he gives sinners the death sentence. It's like a judge in a court of law who sentences a criminal to death for viciously murdering three young girls. The criminal has *earned* the electric chair. This is what he *deserves*; it's his due *wages*.

Let's see what wages you will earn on judgment day. *Do you think you are a good person?* No doubt, like most of us, you do. So I will be your prosecutor, and you be the defendant. Answer my questions with the truth, the whole truth, and nothing but the truth, so help you God, and then you judge yourself as innocent or guilty. Just make sure you are brutally honest, or you will deceive and cheat yourself.

How many lies do you think you have told in your life? This includes "white" lies and half-truths. Have you ever stolen something, even if it was small—irrespective of its value? If you take one dollar out of my wallet, you're as much a thief as if you stole ten dollars. The value of the stolen item is irrelevant. If you've done either of these two things, then you are a sinner.

When authorities put large digital speedometers on the side of the road, it's not for our entertainment. It's to give us a measuring rod so that we can see if we are obeying the law. It shows us exactly how much we have transgressed.

This is what I'm doing with you. I'm showing you a moral speedometer so that you can see how *much* you are in transgression of God's law.

Most don't take any notice of those speedometers on the side of the highway. I have watched motorists speed past them on freeways without slowing down even slightly. However, if there is a police officer sitting on his motorbike beside one of those speedometers, that changes everything. Traffic immediately slows down. This is because they know that the law will be backed by future punishment. It is that knowledge that slows them down.

We are looking at some of the Ten Commandments to see how much you have transgressed God's law. But doing this will mean little to you unless you understand that God backs his law with the promise of future punishment. After we've looked at your transgression, we will look at that threat of divine punishment.

Let's look at the third commandment. Have you ever used God's name in vain, either flippantly (including "OMG") or as profanity? If you have, let me ask you if you would ever use your *mother's* name as a cuss word. I'm sure you wouldn't because that would show you don't respect her in the slightest. And yet you have used God's holy name as a cuss word. That's called *blasphemy*, and it's very serious in God's eyes:

> For they speak against You wickedly;
> Your enemies take Your name in vain.
> (Psalm 139:20)

He promises that whoever takes his name in vain will not be guiltless (see Exodus 20:7).

One more question. Jesus said that if we look with lust we commit adultery in our heart (see Matthew 5:27–28). Have you ever looked with lust at someone? If you're normal, you have. So here is a summation of your court case. You have admitted to being a lying, thieving, blasphemous adulterer at heart. On judgment day, when God judges you by the Ten Commandments, how will you plead—innocent or guilty? Guilty, of course. Will you therefore go to heaven or hell? The answer is frightening. If we die in our sins, we have God's promise that we will end up damned in hell (see Mark 16:16).

BUT EVERYONE SINS

When confronted about our sins, we more often than not try to justify ourselves by saying that *everyone* sins. Or we try to find fault with the Bible. Or we try to separate ourselves from our sins by admitting that we *did* lie or steal, but it was "in the past." However, even human law holds us responsible for crimes done in the past:

The old saying is "you can run, but you can't hide."
It worked for a long time for one prison escapee,
but the FBI finally caught up to him in hiding on
Wednesday. After 46 years, Luis Archuleta was
arrested in New Mexico, and will be returned to
Denver, where he escaped from a prison cell in
1974....Denver Police Chief Paul Pazen said in a
statement. "Many members [of] our community
were hurt by Luis Archuleta's actions. The passing of
time does not erase or excuse his crimes."[15]

Though the man in this example tried to avoid the
consequences of his past actions, they eventually caught up
to him. Rather than think that you can escape your own
mistakes, do yourself the ultimate favor. Don't try to cover
your transgressions or attempt to justify yourself. That
won't work on judgment day. You've *earned* your wages. The
Bible says that all liars will be cast into the lake of fire (see
Revelation 21:8). No thief, no adulterer, and no blasphemer
will inherit the kingdom of God. Does that make you fearful? If it does, that's good. Fear is doing its beneficial work.
It's being your friend, not your enemy—by showing you
that you need God's mercy. You need a parachute before
you pass on into eternity.

---

15   Mark Osborne, "FBI Catches Man 46 Years after He Escaped
from Denver Prison," ABC News (website), August 5, 2020, https://
abcnews.go.com/US/fbi-catches-man-escaped-denver-jail-46-years/
story?id=72204643.

Hopefully, the truth about your sinful condition is humbling you so that you will be able to understand the good news of the gospel—that you *can't* save yourself but that God kindly offers you a parachute in Jesus Christ, the Savior.

The Good News

The Ten Commandments are God's "moral law." You and I broke the law, but Jesus paid the fine with his life's blood. That's what happened when he suffered and died on the cross. That's why he said just before he died, "It is finished!" (John 19:30). In other words, the debt has been paid in full. If you're in court and someone pays your fine, the judge can let you go even though you are guilty. In doing so, he still does what is legal, right, and just. Even though you are guilty, you are free to walk out of the courtroom—because someone has paid your fine.

The Bible says, "God demonstrates His own love toward us, in that while we were still sinners, Christ died for us" (Romans 5:8). God proved his great love for us through the cross. Then Jesus rose from the dead and defeated the power of the grave.

It is because Jesus paid the fine for sin on the cross that God can pardon our crimes. We can walk out of his courtroom on judgment day. He can remove our death sentence and legally let us live forever. All because Jesus paid the fine for sin in full on that cross. Again, he paid the fine, so we can be free from the penalty of death.

God has made the way to find everlasting life so simple that a child can understand it. All you need to do is be honest and humble. You simply have to repent of your sins and trust in Jesus alone for your eternal salvation. Repentance means to *turn* from sin. You can't say you're a Christian and continue to lie, steal, fornicate, lust, and blaspheme God's name. That would be to deceive yourself and play the hypocrite. Your repentance must be sincere to be genuine.

Then you trust in Jesus alone, as you would trust in a parachute. Do you remember what the Bible says to do—"put on the Lord Jesus Christ" (Romans 13:14). The moment you fully trusted in that parachute, you knew the law of gravity no longer had any power over you. In the same way, the moment you put your trust in Jesus for your eternal salvation, the moral law has no power over you: "For the law of the Spirit of life in Christ Jesus has made me free from the law of sin and death" (Romans 8:2).

When we were born into this world, our life began with the corruptible seed of Adam. Sin and death are in our genes. But when we are born again, we are *born of God,* and the seed is therefore incorruptible—which means that death has no part of us: "Having been born again, not of corruptible seed but incorruptible, through the word of God which lives and abides forever" (1 Peter 1:23).

Does that make sense? If it doesn't, reread what I've written until it does *because this is so important*. It's where you will spend eternity. It's the salvation of your soul, which is far more precious than even your physical safety. So today, repent and trust in Jesus because the reality is that you may not have tomorrow.

If you're not sure how to repent, here is a model prayer of repentance, given to us in the Scriptures, when King David had his sin exposed by Nathan the prophet:

> Have mercy upon me, O God,
> According to Your lovingkindness;
> According to the multitude of Your tender mercies,
> Blot out my transgressions.
> Wash me thoroughly from my iniquity,
> And cleanse me from my sin.
> For I acknowledge my transgressions,
> And my sin is always before me
> Against You, You only, have I sinned,
> And done this evil in Your sight—
> That You may be found just when You speak,
> And blameless when You judge. (Psalm 51:1–4)

Whatever you do, don't trust in your own goodness to save you, as most people do. That's like flapping your arms when you jump out of a plane. It's not going to work. You're not a perfect person; you're like the rest of us. Transfer your trust from yourself to the Savior.

We trust doctors and pharmaceutical companies when we take pills, cables when we step into an elevator, and pilots when we fly on planes. Doctors can make mistakes, elevators can let us down, and pilots sometimes make deadly errors. But God will never let you down. He is without sin, and because of that, the Scriptures tell us that it is impossible for him to lie (see Hebrews 6:18). Therefore, trust him with all of your heart, right now. Please, don't put it off for another second.

Then make sure you pick up a Bible, read it daily, and obey what you read. Prayer is us talking to God, but reading the Bible is God speaking to us, and we need to be swift to hear and slow to speak.

Amazing Monopoly

During the Second World War the British government devised a fascinating plan to help prisoners escape from Nazi war camps.

One necessary item for an escape was a reliable map. However, paper maps have some drawbacks: they can be noisy to open and fold, they can fade, the paper can rip, get wet, or wear out.

The brilliant solution was to print maps on silk. Silk is durable, can be silently folded up into tiny portions, and doesn't wear out. In those days there was only one manufacturer in Britain that printed on silk: John Waddington,

Ltd. Coincidentally, they were also the British licensee for "Monopoly," which was permitted in care packages from the International Red Cross to prisoners of war.

Eager to help, and under great secrecy, employees of John Waddington, Ltd., began producing silk escape maps, individualized for each area of Germany, Italy, and France where Allied POW camps were located. The maps were folded and hidden inside Monopoly playing pieces. Employees also added:

1. A tiny magnetic compass
2. A very small two-portion metal file that screwed together
3. German, Italian, and French money

Then British and American air crews were trained on how spot the tiny red dot in the "Free Parking" square, made to look like a printing mistake, that identified these precious Monopoly sets.

The specially equipped Monopoly sets assisted as many as one-third of the Allied POWs who escaped to freedom during the Second World War. Every one of those prisoners was sworn to secrecy because the British Government said that the idea was so effective, they may want to use it again in the event of another war. This story didn't become public knowledge until 2007, at which time those still living who were involved with creating the sets received public honors for their efforts.[16]

---

16   David Mikkelson, "Were Escape Kits Smuggled to WWII POWs in

The gospel is the secret map that tells us how to escape death, and it is hidden from the proud (something we will look at more closely in the next chapter). Jesus said, "I thank You, Father, Lord of heaven and earth, that You have hidden these things from the wise and prudent and have revealed them to babes" (Matthew 11:25).

Today, I hope that you have a humble and honest heart and that the gospel has therefore shown you how to escape the clutches of death.

Remember, the fear of death should be your protector. Every day we hear of tragedies befalling people who didn't listen to that God-given friend and instead laughed in its face—by doing dangerous extreme sports or speeding on motorbikes and in cars. Graveyards are filled with such foolish people. Be wise. Listen to it, and it will not only send you to him who saves from death, but it will also keep you from death's clutches.

I thank God for the horror that I felt when I stood hopeless and helpless before the grim reaper. But now that the Lord is my helper and I have a living hope in Christ—an anchor for my soul—I never let myself forget that tormenting fear. Now and then I allow it to take my breath away so that I remember what it was like to live without hope. That makes me not only appreciate the glorious hope I have in Jesus, but it also keeps me from toying with the pleasures of sin, which I now know is the very cause of death. Now you also know the happy truth of salvation. How are you going to respond? In the next chapter, we will look at a few examples of poor responses to the reality of death and the truth of God's gift of salvation.

Words of Comfort

> Have I not commanded you? Be strong and of good
> courage; do not be afraid, nor be dismayed, for the
> Lord your God is with you wherever you go.
> (Joshua 1:9)

This is what God himself said to Joshua. He commanded
him to 1.) Be strong. 2.) Be of good courage. 3.) Not be
afraid. And 4.) Not be dismayed. Why? Because God was
with him wherever he went.

From the moment we find peace with God we need
never fear or be dismayed because Jesus will never leave us
nor forsake us no matter how great the storm. We have his
immutable promise on that. It's just a matter of us believing it:

> "Go therefore and make disciples of all the nations,
> baptizing them in the name of the Father and of
> the Son and of the Holy Spirit, teaching them to
> observe all things that I have commanded you;
> *and lo, I am with you always, even to the end of the
> age." Amen.* (Matthew 28:19–20, emphasis added)

CHAPTER SIX

SOLOMON'S CONCLUSION

A man with curly, black, shoulder-length hair was sitting at the base of a tree along with his skateboard and a small dog on his lap. I asked him if I could talk to him about the afterlife on camera for our YouTube channel, and after a little arm twisting, Salvador gave his permission.

My first question was, "What are your thoughts on the afterlife?" He quickly responded saying, "That's a topic a lot of people choose to ignore. There's stuff that I've seen that I can't explain. And there just *has* to be something else at the end. I really don't feel that life is just you wake up every day, you go to work until you get tired. It's a never-ending cycle of go to work every day. You go home. You dream. You have hopes..." He then ran out of words to express his frustration. I was taken aback by what he said. It was as though I was listening to myself, forty-eight years ago.

I asked, "Have you heard of King Solomon?" He hadn't. I continued, "He wrote a substantial part of the Bible. And one of the portions he wrote is called *Ecclesiastes*. He said that all is vanity. It's like chasing the wind. You go to work, you come home (I'm paraphrasing), you get old, you die. What's the point?" Salvador nodded in agreement as I spoke.

The Scriptures tell us that King Solomon asked God for wisdom, and God certainly gave it to him. And the summation of his wisdom was that life (without a knowledge of salvation) is utterly futile. He had attainted great power and immeasurable riches, and yet with all his power, wisdom, and wealth, he said that life is like running after the wind. And this futility exists all because of one thing. Humanity's impending death.

The obvious conclusion from Solomon's writings is that those who don't fear death, don't think. They are shallow in their thoughts about the precious nature of life. Solomon identifies those as ones who exist to "discover" their own heart (see Proverbs 18:2). The empty-headed hedonist's philosophy is to eat, drink, and be merry, for tomorrow he dies. Squeeze happiness out of life before it's over. But the wise aren't happy with temporal squeezing. They don't want to party on the Titanic. They are looking for a lifeboat.

Solomon didn't have a lifeboat, but he pointed us in the right direction by telling us to fear God—and those who fear God will end up at the foot of the cross. Those who don't won't.

He begins his philosophical thesis with:

> "Vanity of vanities," says the Preacher;
> "Vanity of vanities, all is vanity."
> What profit has a man from all his labor
> In which he toils under the sun?
> One generation passes away, and another
> generation comes;
> But the earth abides forever. (Ecclesiastes 1:2–4)

He saw life as a tedious and endless procession of sunrises, sunsets, rain, snow, wind, and seasons. They come and go, and finally, death comes and ends the repetitive futility.

Then he gives his testimony:

> I communed with my heart, saying, "Look, I have attained greatness, and have gained more wisdom than all who were before me in Jerusalem. My heart has understood great wisdom and knowledge." And I set my heart to know wisdom and to know madness and folly. I perceived that this also is grasping for the wind.
> For in much wisdom is much grief,
> And he who increases knowledge increases sorrow. (Ecclesiastes 1:16–18)

His depressing worldview existed because he had wisdom and knowledge. The shallow thinker skips joyfully through a field of flowers and silently disappears over a thousand-foot cliff. He knows it's coming, but like a thoughtless little child, he keeps skipping toward the cliff anyway. Solomon wanted to avoid it. Wisdom brings us to grief and sorrow—and hopefully grief and sorrow bring us to the Savior. Both of these emotions over life's futility were the two catalysts that sent tears down my cheeks back in 1971, and in doing so, they steered me to Jesus. So every time Solomon speaks depressing words of impending death, he is giving us light that will steer us.

He then gets to his point:

> No one has power over the spirit to retain the spirit,
> And no one has power in the day of death.
> There is no release from that war,
> And wickedness will not deliver those who are given to it. (Ecclesiastes 8:8)

We are soldiers marching to a battle that will defeat us. And there's no discharge from that war. He says,

> All things come alike to all:
> One event happens to the righteous and the wicked;
> To the good, the clean, and the unclean;
> To him who sacrifices and him who does
> not sacrifice.
> As is the good, so is the sinner;
> He who takes an oath as he who fears an oath.
> This is an evil in all that is done under the sun: that one thing happens to all. Truly the hearts of the sons

of men are full of evil; madness is in their hearts
while they live, and after that they go to the dead.
(Ecclesiastes 9:2–3)

Listen to this wisest of men. Glean from his wisdom.
He is reminding us (from the grave) that death is imminent. But you have a great advantage over Solomon. You
know the gospel. *You know the way of salvation.* What are
you going to do about it?

WHY THE WORLD DOESN'T UNDERSTAND

A popular movie from 1950 called *Summer Stock* (starring
Phil Silvers, Gene Kelly, and Judy Garland—then household
names) showed a group of playactors who were about to be
evicted. As they sat in a group, comedian Phil Silvers suddenly raised his hands and addressed Gene Kelly as if he was
a gospel preacher. He, in a mocking southern accent, said,

> I hear your message brother! Show me the way.
> You're wise and you're good...I want to be saved. Save
> me. Save me! Ain't that the truth? Are you listening
> to the man? This is the man that saved me. I was
> wicked...but this is the man that showed me the way.
> This is the man that took me by the hand up to the
> glory room. This is the man that showed me the
> light...this is the man who made me righteous.

It was supposed to be funny because no one needs "saving." To be saved, you need to be in danger, and to shallow-thinking Hollywood screenwriters, there is no danger at all. But Phil Silvers was cut down by the grim reaper in 1985. Death took Gene Kelly in 1996, and Judy Garland died in 1969 at the age of forty-seven due to a drug overdose. The writers of the mocking script are also dead. George Wells died in the year 2000, and death took out Sy Gomberg in 2001.

This raises the question of why any human being who has a love of life would mock the message of how to be saved from death. The answer is simple. It's because the good news of the gospel is hidden from the proud.

A proud heart doesn't want to look weak by getting into a lifeboat, and he mocks those who do. Jesus is the only lifeboat God offers drowning humanity. He's the only one who can save us from death and damnation. To mock him is to bite the divine hand that feeds us, and that reveals that we are not wise.

This pride becomes clear when people are faced with the gospel and refuse to acknowledge their sin. When I'm about to take someone through the Ten Commandments, I usually ask, "Can you be honest with me?" Then I listen carefully. If they refuse to admit that they've broken the Commandments, I know that they're going to miss the glorious gospel. They will unwittingly trample pearls in mud beneath their feet. To that which is most precious, they won't give even the slightest value.

This is because if a man has a disease but refuses to acknowledge the evident symptoms, he won't appreciate a cure. Why should he want a cure when he doesn't think he even has the disease? But if he is honest and admits to the symptoms and that he will die because of the disease, he will greatly value the cure.

When someone lacks honesty about their sins, I know he's going to be blind to the good news of everlasting life. It will go over his head and be hidden from his understanding.

What about you? How did you react when the light of God's law came to you? Were you brutally honest about your sins? Did you bring them to the light, or did you try to cover them by justifying yourself? Oh, the terrible remorse you will have if you die in your sins. You will think back to this very moment—when you came so close to escaping hell and finding heaven, but you crept back into the darkness. Please, don't let that happen.

HERE'S AN EXAMPLE

Let's see an example of a man who was very familiar with the good news but rejected it out of a refusal to admit to his own sin. I've had many discussions with atheists. Atheists who would like to talk with me about God can do so via video.

However, they must first explain why they would like to talk. One man (we will call him "John") wrote the following:

I am a graduate of the Abeka school system, which I used from first through twelfth grade, as well as of Pensacola Christian College. I attended PCC from 2005 through 2010 and gained a Bachelor of Arts in church music with a minor in Bible studies.

I was very active in my home church from birth through college, participating in every church activity (choir, teaching, VBS, door-to-door witnessing, camps, weekly grounds work, internship, etc.).

I had a few standard salvation and assurance experiences starting at age six at my uncle's church (he is a pastor). I was brought to tears every time I read about the crucifixion, heard a sermon on the Passion Week, or read/watched *The Lion, the Witch, and the Wardrobe*.

I witnessed to my coworkers at the factory where I worked during high school. I read my KJV Bible there daily and brought at least one person to salvation and church membership.

I became a music teacher at a Christian school with fellow PCC alumni in Louisville, KY. I witnessed to people I would meet from Saudi Arabia and other countries. I once received a package of clothes from Saudi Arabia from a Muslim family that they sent out of gratitude to me for sharing my faith with them.

While growing up, I was a big fan of Ray Comfort and Kent Hovind and then of *Answers in Genesis* ministries. I met family and friends of Hovind at college and still have them as friends on Facebook.

After my brother started questioning his faith, I decided I would engage with atheism online to understand and dismantle it. I lost my faith after the first video I watched, and since then I have seen every piece of content from or about Hitchens, Harris, Dawkins, Denney, Dillahunty, Atheist Experience (AE), and many others.[17]

In other words, John was a sincere and committed Christian who believed he had discovered that God wasn't real.

Here's someone else who fell away from the faith:

I followed Jesus for more than three years and was so trusted by my fellow believers that I was put in charge of the financial side of the ministry. When I saw extravagance, I expressed my convictions that, as believers, we should care for the poor. My faith was so strong, I prayed for the sick and saw so-called miracles of healing. But in time I realized that there

---

17   This message has been edited for readability.

were more important things in life than following Jesus, so I made a decision to betray him.
—Judas Iscariot

There have been millions, who, just like John, have made a decision to follow Jesus and in time have fallen away, and some (like John) try and convince others that they are as deceived as they once were. But their words are nothing but a thin smokescreen. They didn't fall away because God isn't real but because they loved their sin. This was also the case with Judas (see John 12:4–6).

John's Defense

A criminal stands in court charged with a serious crime. The evidence of his guilt is indisputable. But instead of admitting his guilt, he attempts to discredit the law that justly accuses him. He did rob a bank and shoot a guard, but his defense is that the human brain is neurologically designed to want to rob banks and to shoot authority figures such as guards. He is therefore guiltless.

In the face of the law's just accusations against his evident sin, John pleaded that we was not responsible. Here is a transcript of our online conversation (slightly edited for readability). I asked John: "You've watched a number of videos. How do you measure up to the Commandments?"

> JOHN: Hmmm. Which Commandments are you referring to?

RAY: Well, when did you last look at pornography?

JOHN: Well, I'm interested because you mentioned the Commandments. Are you referring to the Ten Commandments or are you referring to the commandments that were smashed before the Ten Commandments were given? Because the actual Ten Commandments were given...they were the ones that include not boiling a goat in its mother's milk.

Three times the Scriptures state: "You shall not boil a kid in its mother's milk" (Exodus 23:19, 34:26; Deuteronomy 14:21). The command "was connected with the Passover which may indicate that this was a mystical and unacceptable practice which is considered 'unclean' and unwholesome. Archaeologists have discovered texts in ancient Syria that explain that boiling a sacrifice of a young goat in their mother's milk was a ritual practice of the Canaanites."[18]

The ceremonial law instructed Israel not to imitate the wicked customs of surrounding nations (particularly the Canaanites). John tried to discount the law by saying that the ceremonial law was part of the moral law. The ceremonial laws were given solely to the nation of Israel, but the moral law was and is directed at the entire world

---

18 "What Does the Verse 'You Shall Not Boil a Young Goat in Its Mother's Milk' Mean?," BibleAsk, accessed on September 20, 2020, https://bibleask.org/what-does-the-verse-you-shall-not-boil-a-young-goat-in-its-mothers-milk-mean/.

(see Romans 3:19, 20; Romans 2:12; James 2:12). John was saying that the law that accused him was trivial and non-sensical—because it included an ordinance about boiling kids in goat's milk—and it was therefore irrelevant. I have heard many others try to redirect commandments to free themselves from their condemnation.

> JOHN: That's the Ten Commandments. I've never done that because when the Bible says these Ten Commandments, it's referring to the list that ends in not boiling a goat in its mother's milk. It says, "These are the Ten Commandments."
>
> RAY: Yeah. Really good. John, it's Exodus 20. The Ten Commandments in Exodus 20. So back to the question at hand, this is the seventh commandment, where Jesus said if you look at a woman and lust for her, you commit adultery with her in your heart.
>
> JOHN: It's the seventh commandment of the list that was smashed before the Ten Commandments were given.

Do you remember the original question I asked John? It was, "When did you last look at pornography?" He was trying to dodge it because it came as a curveball. It's easy to lie when asked, "*Do* you look at pornography?" That's a yes-or-no question, making it easy to lie. But "When did you *last* look at pornography?" carries an assumption—and the assumption is justified. This is because people take to sexual

sin as a duck goes to water. The Scriptures even say that we
drink iniquity like we do water (see Job 15:16). We can't live
without water, and sinful human beings cannot live without
sin. We are addicted to it because it gives us life. Jesus said
that if we serve sin, we are a slave to it (see John 8:34). The
Bible doesn't say that we have just a propensity to sin or
that we simply like it. It says that we *love* it: "And this is the
condemnation, that the light has come into the world, *and
men loved darkness* rather than light, because their deeds
were evil" (John 3:19, emphasis added).

John thought that he had avoided the curveball, so I
threw it at him once again. This time a little harder.

RAY: Okay, so when did you last look at
pornography?

JOHN: Ah. That question is, um, it's a question
that I think is getting at our actions, our drives, our
personality, what our motivations and our actions....I
think those are governed by...the overwhelming
evidence suggests our actions are, our behaviors
are governed by the neurological...Evidence suggests it's determined by our biology, by our brain
chemistry, by what's going on up in here [he points
to his head]. Sam Harris and others have given a
strong case for, um, several evidence that when you
damage the brain, your actions are determined, and
if you damage certain parts of the brain, it can make
you more aggressive...If you're born with certain

malformations, there's lots of evidence that suggests that our actions are determined by our brain, and there is, there is little to no forensic data, biological, physical evidence that suggests that your ability to choose is determined by anything that would be considered by will of your own, and in any case, whatever your ability to choose is governed by. You didn't choose it because you were given the cards that you have before you were born. And so that's...so my perspective as far as your ability to be accountable for your actions would be that your, your actions are determined by what's going on in your brain.

RAY: So when did you last look at pornography?

JOHN: Sir, I'm not gonna answer that question. It's of a sexual, personal nature, and I don't think it's any of your business.

John only needed to say, "I don't look at pornography," and the case would have been closed. Or he could have simply said, "There's nothing wrong with pornography because with atheists, there's no absolute moral standard of right and wrong. I look at it regularly like millions of others. It's no big deal."

But he didn't. He instead tried to discredit God's law, and then he tried to justify himself. This is because he had discounted the power of his latent conscience.

Our conscience, even though it can be dulled to sleep when we sin, is stirred from its slumber when the moral law is cited. It echoes the truth of the Ten Commandments. We intuitively know that it's wrong to lie, to steal, to murder, to commit adultery, and we inherently know that it's morally wrong to look with lust. Just before I came to Christ, a friend came around to our house and asked me to come to the driveway (away from my wife). He then showed me some Swedish pornography. And even though my godless eyes bulged with delight, I will never forget that my conscience *screamed* at me. I knew I was displeasing God, even though I had been left without any parental godly instruction.

Look closely at these verses and how they give insight as to what happens in our hearts when the moral law does its accusatory work:

> When Gentiles, who do not have the Law [since it was given only to Jews], do instinctively the things the Law requires [guided only by their conscience], they are a law to themselves, though they do not have the Law. They show that the essential requirements of the Law are written in their hearts; and their conscience [their sense of right and wrong, their moral choices] bearing witness and their thoughts alternately accusing or perhaps defending them on that day when, as my gospel proclaims, God will judge the secrets [all the hidden thoughts and concealed sins] of men through Christ Jesus. (Romans 2:14–16 AMP)

What should you say to someone like John? Some would say to leave him alone, and I would do that if I didn't care about his terrifying fate if he died in his sins. But I couldn't let him go without pleading with him to come to his senses. Here is the last part of our conversation:

JOHN: If atheism is an attempt to escape God—an intentional attempt to escape God—that would mean that those who don't accept your doctrine before they die are intentionally endangering their own children by not accepting that doctrine.

RAY: How?

JOHN: Because they would be not encouraging their children to avoid eternal damnation, intentionally.

RAY: I would probably be an atheist if I had your theology. Any person's salvation comes from the sovereignty of God. God saves whom he wills, when he wills. He reaches out to the whole of mankind, but we so love sin that we refuse to come to him. It takes his grace to draw us to himself. You know that "No man comes to the Son unless the Father draws him."

JOHN: Are you referring to Calvin? Are you referring to Calvinism? Are you a Calvinist?

RAY: No. I'm referring to Jesus. He said no man comes to the Son unless the Father draws him. I've never read Calvin. I've never quoted Calvin, so I'm not a Calvinist. I'm just saying what the Bible says.

SOLOMON'S CONCLUSION ～ 85

We are so rebellious, we are so sin-loving, that it takes God's mercy and his grace to draw us to himself. And he can do that with your children despite your will. If you don't care about them, he does. He wants them saved.

You don't really care because you love your sins. And that's as basic as I can get. "Open rebuke is better than a secret love." I'm not going to tickle your ears. I'm going to say, "John, I love you." I care about you. I'm going to tell the truth. I love you. Your family loves you. You're grieving them by your love of sin. You're looking at pornography and not admitting it. It's obvious. I've asked literally hundreds of guys, "Are you looking at pornography?" and they say, "Sure, all the time. I love it." They don't say, "That's a deeply personal question about peoples' genitalia." No, it's just straight, "I love my sin, and I'm choosing it. I'm choosing death and hell and damnation. I'm just carrying on doing what I'm doing because I love atheism"—which is scientifically impossible.

Man, I've talked to so many atheists, and they say the same silly things—goats' milk and all that stuff from the Hebrew nation, what, three thousand years ago? They find little nitpicking things when the issue is that death is going to seize them. We've found everlasting life. I want them to be saved. They couldn't care less because they love their sins. And I want you to *please* think about that.

I can't teach you anything. You've been brought up in a Christian family. You've been brought up in a church. You know the truth. All I can do is say to you, "Man, you've had a false conversion. Please think about your eternity." If you died tonight, it will bring tears to my heart, and it grieves me. So my motive (I don't know what your motive is for talking to me), but my motive for talking to you is because I love you. I care about you. I want to see you saved. And you've had a false conversion, and the churches are full of them. And I deal with them all the time, and they are the hardest to reach.

So I'd be grateful if you would take the time to watch "Crazy Bible" and see if I've edited things deceitfully. I don't think I have; it's very clear what these guys say. And then just weigh up what your beliefs are. Because your beliefs will govern your steps. If you believe there's a landmine in front of you, you'll go around the landmine. If you don't believe, you go right onto it. So your beliefs are very important; they're your convictions, especially about your eternity.

Hey, I've been chatting for thirty-five minutes. I've really got to go. I've got things on this morning, but I really appreciate you talking to me.

JOHN: Absolutely. I appreciate your time, sir.
Have a good day, sir. Thank you.

I was so thankful that he listened and that I had his
conscience on my side. My prayer was that his conscience
would do its God-given duty and confirm the truths I had
shared with him.

REMEMBER NOW

How depressing this life would be without the gospel. Solomon had a glimmer of its light, but we have its full sunlight.
He shared what light he had by telling those who are young
to look past the pleasures of life and remember God and his
demands:

> Remember now your Creator in the days of
> your youth,
> Before the difficult days come,
> And the years draw near when you say,
> "I have no pleasure in them." (Ecclesiastes 12:1)

He then brings his wisdom to a wonderful conclusion:

> Let us hear the conclusion of the whole matter:
> Fear God and keep His commandments,
> For this is man's all.
> For God will bring every work into judgment,
> Including every secret thing,
> Whether good or evil. (Ecclesiastes 12:13–14)

How amazing, that God made provision for our sin! As a Christian, I no longer fear when I know that God will "bring every work to judgment." This is because I'm trusting in Jesus' work instead of my own. Is that your testimony? I certainly hope so.

God will bring every work into judgment. That should put the fear of God into us, and the fear of God should bring us to the Savior. It is there that death loses its sting and vanity is shattered forever.

WORDS OF COMFORT

> For God has not given us a spirit of fear, but of
> power and of love and of a sound mind.
> (2 Timothy 1:7)

When we come to the Savior, God gives us his Holy Spirit.
Look now at the evidence of having the Holy Spirit in
our lives:

> But the fruit of the Spirit is love, joy, peace, long-
> suffering, kindness, goodness, faithfulness, gentle-
> ness, self-control. Against such there is no law. And
> those who are Christ's have crucified the flesh with
> its passions and desires. If we live in the Spirit, let us
> also walk in the Spirit. (Galatians 5:22–25)

Fear isn't part of our new life in Christ. It's to be cruci-
fied along with sinful passions that will destroy us. Put fear
to death daily.

CHAPTER SEVEN

WHEN GOD DOESN'T ANSWER

To say that the Christian life is a bed of roses is to be disingenuous. There are also thorns. Lots of them. The Bible says that we enter the kingdom of God through much tribulation (see Acts 14:22). The Christian life is so full of trials that they often bring us to our knees. And that's the safest place for Christian to be. Once we've trusted in Jesus for salvation from our sins and deliverance from death, we need to continue trusting in him for help with the daily struggles of life. Someone wisely said that trusting in Jesus doesn't mean a smooth flight, but it does mean a safe landing. I would, therefore, like to share with you some biblical principles on how to deal with the turbulence that comes with daily living as a Christian.

Whenever I hear Sue call, "Can you help me?" I stop whatever I'm doing and quickly respond. Often, it's just to move a heavy potted plant or hammer in a nail with which she's having trouble. Her will is my priority because our marriage isn't only held together by law; it's held together by love. My wife isn't merely my legal spouse. She's my best friend, and friends always respond indeed when a friend is in need.

Before the new birth, it's easy to imagine that God is our friend and to treat him like one. We tell him our wants and needs. But without genuine faith, we will eventually feel let down because when tragedy strikes, he doesn't respond as we think he should—the divine friend doesn't show up when he's needed. Friends and family get sick and die despite earnest prayer for their health and recovery. Many in the world understandably become disillusioned, and some become bitter against God for his supposed inaction.

In John chapter 11 the Scriptures give us an incident where a supposed friend didn't come running, and there was potential for bitterness. A man named Lazarus became very sick. His two sisters were so concerned for his well-being that they sent an urgent message to Jesus, saying that their beloved brother was ill. It was because Jesus loved their brother that he would, without question, come and heal him. They knew that he had healed strangers before, and this was certainly a case worthy of his attention. And there was the added incentive that Lazarus was a good friend.

Their message was simple, "Lord, behold, he whom You love is sick" (John 11:3). No more needed to be said. They had even included the word "Behold." Someone once said that that word in the Bible was used as a trumpet blast. It heralded something of great significance. It was saying, "Listen up." And they were saying that to Jesus: "Listen up! Your friend is extremely sick."

It was certainly true about the love that Jesus had for Lazarus. He not only loved him, but he also loved the two sisters—Mary and Martha—and that gave even more reason for him to drop whatever he was doing and come running. But that didn't happen. Instead we are told, "So, when He heard that he was sick, He stayed two more days in the place where He was" (John 11:6).

He did the unthinkable. He heard that his beloved friend was sick, and he deliberately stayed where he was for two more days. Perhaps there was some sort of misunderstanding. Maybe he didn't realize how ill Lazarus was, or he was involved in something more important and he couldn't respond.

But there was no misunderstanding. Neither was there something more important that kept him where he was. Jesus both acknowledged the friendship, and he knew that the illness was as deadly as an illness could get:

> These things He said, and after that He said to them, "Our friend Lazarus sleeps, but I go that I may wake him up." Then His disciples said, "Lord, if he

sleeps he will get well." However, Jesus spoke of his death, but they thought that He was speaking about taking rest in sleep. Then Jesus said to them plainly, "Lazarus is dead. And I am glad for your sakes that I was not there, that you may believe. Nevertheless let us go to him." (John 11:11–15)

LIFE-SAVING INSTRUCTIONS

If you are in a hotel room, it is wise to take a moment to read the information that has been placed on the back of the door by which you enter. It will show you how to get out of the building in case of fire. I have stayed in hundreds of different hotel rooms, and the way of escape is always different.

Personally, I don't always care to read instructions. I have what I consider to be more important things on my mind. I have to speak at a dinner and have to look over my notes, change my clothes, call my wife. But experts tell us that in a massive fire where there are multiple floors in a hotel, smoke can be so thick you can't see where you are going, and just one breath of carcinogen-filled smoke can cause you to pass out and perish in the flames. So I have to make an effort to check the location of the exit in case of fire. It's common knowledge that the only place where there is breathable air is low to the floor, and knowing that I have to turn left twice and then right once, and how far to walk in blinding smoke to find the exit can mean the difference between life and death.

Those who are wise will *make* time to quickly read information that could potentially save their lives in a new hotel. The information I'm about to give you is just as important. Temporarily put every other concern aside, and please make it a priority to listen up.

The story of Lazarus gives us the first principle of the Christian life: keeping low through a humble heart and having trust is the oxygen that that keeps us alive in Christ. Without it, we cannot please God (see Hebrews 11:6). Without faith, we can't even please people. Try not trusting someone and see if you keep your friendship. Say to your best friend, "I don't have faith in you," and watch the friendship go sour. Faith is the glue that holds relationships together.

When "Lazarus" experiences come our way, we must keep our trust in God. Like every other Christian, I have gone for months, and sometimes for years, without God answering my prayers in a way I think he should. I've asked for something, and he did what Jesus did when Lazarus was sick. There was no response when I needed one. Fortunately, I have had the knowledge (from Scripture) that tells me that this is often the way God works. I know that he loves me. The cross is an everlasting reminder of that, but I also know that more often than not, he has a bigger and better purpose in mind than I do. He sees the future, and he sees the end result. I merely see the present persistent pressing problem. Faith helps me to look beyond it. It lifts me onto my toes so I can see over it.

IT FELT FAMILIAR

Let me share a "Lazarus" experience with you to illustrate this important point.

I was sitting in our television studio doing some recording for the Spanish Division of our ministry when I felt a pain on my lower left side of my back. It felt vaguely familiar. About twenty-eight years earlier I had a similar pain that turned out to be a kidney stone that I fortunately passed a day or so later.

We were having a short break from filming, and we planned to get back into it. All that was needed from me was a short commendation of our Spanish Division that would be translated into Spanish. But the pain became so unbearable I had to get out of the studio.

I went into our board room and closed the door. Over the next forty minutes, I was beside myself with pain. Then it left, and I was back to normal. I did a little filming, and then I went to a local college to interview people for our YouTube channel.

About five days later the pain started again. This was just as intense, and as time passed, it became so bad that I said to Sue that I needed to go to the hospital. The pain intensified to a point where I wanted to tell her to stop the

car so that I could get out and lie on the sidewalk. This
would become a common desire over the next week. I
found that others, including my daughter-in-law who had
experienced a kidney stone, once lay helplessly on the sidewalk outside of the emergency room.

We finally made it to the ER, checked in, and filled out
forms as we sat in the waiting room. But I couldn't sit still;
I went into the parking lot and leaned against trees, walked
around, and cried out to God for help. Suddenly, I heard
someone calling my name. It was my turn to see the doctor.
We went through a standard procedure of questions about
my height and weight, background, and age, and then they
put me into a bed. I was still in intense pain until somebody came, examined me, gave me a shot of morphine, and
wheeled me off to have a CAT scan.

On the way to get the scan, I was able to share the gospel with the young man who pushed my gurney. But after
we got back to my room, the pain came back, and they gave
me another shot of morphine. That only lasted for fifteen
minutes, so they gave me a third shot, which predictably
didn't last very long. They then prescribed a drug called
Toradol, which gave me immediate relief.

The CAT scan revealed a five-millimeter kidney stone.
I was then put on a saline solution to fill me with liquid to
try and push it out.

After that, they sent me home with a powerful drug
called Norco. I was to take one every six hours. When the

pain started, that's what I did. But there was no relief, and I didn't dare take a second one. I didn't realize that Norco was an opiate that had bad side effects. One was that it altered the taste buds. A plate of my favorite cereal tasted like dishwashing liquid, and a mere breath mint tasted disgusting.

That night the pain became so intense (as I lay on the floor crying) that Sue called an ambulance. Within minutes there were six tall paramedics surrounding me as I sat on the floor in our living room—asking questions as to the intensity of the pain and other incidentals.

During the trip to the hospital the pain thankfully subsided, and I was able to share the gospel with a young man named Brett. He was the consummate paramedic you'd see on a television show—tall, handsome, and very compassionate. He also turned out to be a liar, a thief, a blasphemer, and an adulterer at heart. He was clearly feeling the heat of the law and kept touching the screen of his laptop, as though he was busy doing something more important than what we were talking about. But when I talked to him about the fact that he was surrounded by death (and that death was evidence that God was serious about sin), he began looking at me and listening to my every word. Then he said that his best friend was a very committed Christian. I told Brett that he was listening because of his friend's prayers. It was a good time.

After a two-hour wait in a hospital corridor, I was again examined, given some Toradol, and then sent home with some more Norco.

I began to see a pattern. I would have temporary relief for up to seven hours because of the drug, and then the pain would come back. I would moan a little as I sat in my chair (for about five minutes) and then have to go into another room. There, I would lie on the floor. Then I would begin groaning and hyperventilating, cry with pain, and then ask God to take me home.

Around that time, I made a short YouTube video and said that I had a kidney stone. The response was wonderful. Hundreds said that they were praying for me, and among the comments on the channel I found some sort of consolation:

"I had kidney stones so bad they literally almost killed me! The pain was worse than labor, and my biggest baby was over eleven pounds."

"I had to have a stone removed last year. I've had four children....The stone was worse."

"Kidney stones make childbirth feel like a pleasant experience. I have had four stones and have given birth with no epidural three times. The stones were immeasurably more painful."

On the fourth trip to the ER, a young doctor in the emergency room felt pity for me and transferred me into the hospital to be examined by a urologist with the possibility of having surgery. I spent the night in the hospital, excited to see the urologist and talk about the possibility of removing the stone. I finally had some hope.

At around eight a.m., a doctor walked into my room and with a cold tone told me that he was discharging me. He said that I had a kidney stone and that I was to go home and pass it. He then said that a urologist could do nothing for me. He then walked out and in came a nurse who removed the IV for the pain killer. My hope of relief was gone. I was sent home with a bottle of Norco.

Earlier I had asked the doctor if they were strict about taking one Norco every six hours. He said that I could take two every four hours. That was a huge relief, and I no longer felt trapped in the cycle of pain. I could find relief by taking two tablets of this very strong opiate.

It was now Monday evening. When an attack came, I took two Norco tablets and went to bed. As Sue drifted off to sleep, the pain became so intense that I secretly called one of my sons, and I asked him to take me to the ER. Two tablets had done nothing. I didn't want to steal another night's sleep from my dear wife. She was exhausted and frustrated by seeing her husband lying on the floor so often in tears.

This was my fifth ER trip in three days. Once again the pain was so intense that I went into the parking lot and walked around like a wounded animal, crying out for God to come and help me. His good friend was really sick, and he wasn't doing anything. I was helpless, hopeless, and very desperate. Then I suddenly saw the face of my precious daughter walking toward me in the darkness of the parking lot. I ran to her, fell into her arms sobbing like a baby.

Rachel had left her husband and five kids at home to come to me and be my advocate. She had heard that I had been kicked out from the hospital room, and she came with the attitude of a mama grizzly bear. When my name was finally called to go through the form-filling process of my height, my age, and other personal information, she stepped forward. When the doctor said that he was going to send me home with some Norco, she said that it didn't work and that they needed to put me into a hospital to see a urologist. When the young doctor stood up against her, she refused to back down. Mama bear stood on her hind legs.

It was obvious that Mr. Cold-Doctor had chewed him out for giving me a hospital bed the night before. But Rachel wouldn't back down, and he finally conceded to putting me in a bed in the ER under observation, and he would proscribe what he said was another powerful drug.

About an hour later, in came a nurse, and when she went to give me this new drug, mama bear stopped her and asked what she was giving me. It was Norco. Rachel sent her back to her station and went to see the young doctor.

I was finally given some Toradol, and after an hour or so, we received a visit from the boss. This man was in charge of the ER, and he was extremely reasonable. After hearing Rachel argue my case, he said that he was going to put me in a bed in the hospital upstairs but added that they still had the authority to send me home. We found out later that he had gone ahead and booked a urologist, which made it less likely for them to send me home.

After a night in the hospital, Sue came to see me. Rachel then went home, and her husband, E.Z., the president of our ministry, suddenly showed up at the door of the hospital room. I could hardly believe my eyes. He was sharply dressed but looked intimidating at the same time. He was way overdressed for a hospital visit because he had come prepared to chew out Mr. Cold-Doctor before he once again discharged me. E.Z. had already been mistaken for being a doctor when he entered the hospital, and when a nurse saw him sitting on a chair in my room, she immediately wheeled in a recliner. That's because he was obviously someone of great importance.

He never saw the cold doctor—which was fortunate for him because E.Z. is the most eloquent man I know and he wouldn't have minced his words. He even gave me a synopsis of what he had planned to say. If he had bumped into the doctor, I would have filmed it because it would have been a matchless verbal takedown.

Later that morning, in walked the long-expected urologist. He explained my options to Sue, E.Z., and me. He said that I could either go home and pass the stone, or he could operate. But the operation was very complex, and it could give me a stroke or a heart attack—in other words, things could go terribly wrong, and they may not be able to even get the stone. Then he told me about a friend whose wife was the president of a hospital. He said that his friend had chosen to go home and pass the stone rather than have the operation. I looked at the urologist and asked, "Would you have an operation or go home?" He said, "I would go home."

I felt physically sick at the thought of once again going home and then ending up back in the ER. I was between a rock and a hard place, and Jesus still wasn't responding. Where was he in all this? He said that if I had faith, I could tell a *mountain* to be removed, and it would be done. Here's that promise:

> Jesus answered and said to them, "Have faith in God. For assuredly, I say to you, whoever says to this mountain, 'Be removed and be cast into the sea,' and does not doubt in his heart, but believes that those things he says will be done, he will have whatever he says. Therefore I say to you, whatever things you ask when you pray, believe that you receive them, and you will have them." (Mark 11:22–24)

I wasn't doubting. But I was desperate. Besides, I wasn't asking God to remove a mountain. Just a tiny stone. And it wasn't happening. But it didn't shake my faith because I had read the life-saving instructions behind the hotel door. I knew how God works.

E.Z. took a moment to call a godly urologist friend, who said that I should have the operation. Sue said that I should have it. E.Z. said that I should have it. And so we went ahead and scheduled an operation for early that afternoon.

Later that day, as Sue sat in the waiting room, she was approached by one of the surgeons. He sat next to her and told her that my operation had been a failure. They couldn't get the stone. This was because it was impacted. The doctor said that in thirty years of practice, he had only seen three or four impacted stones. He also said that I had made the right decision about having an operation because that stone would not have passed.

I ended up having four surgeries. I will spare you the sordid details, but on the fourth surgery, they finally got it. That little stone cost the insurance company about $100,000, and it cost me and my family time, a great deal of inconvenience, and a lot of pain. All I could see was a massive immovable stone. But let me roll it away and show what was behind it.

Back in John 11:2, we read, "It was that Mary who anointed the Lord with fragrant oil and wiped His feet with her hair, whose brother Lazarus was sick."

This incident is related in chapter 12. This happened after Jesus arrived, and as we will see in the next chapter, Lazarus was raised from the dead. It took place *after* Mary

realized that her disappointment in Jesus wasn't justified.
Here is the passage:

> Six days before the Passover, Jesus came to Bethany,
> where Lazarus was who had been dead, whom He
> had raised from the dead. There they made Him a
> supper; and Martha served, but Lazarus was one of
> those who sat at the table with Him. Then Mary took
> a pound of very costly oil of spikenard, anointed the
> feet of Jesus, and wiped His feet with her hair. And
> the house was filled with the fragrance of the oil. But
> one of His disciples, Judas Iscariot, Simon's son, who
> would betray Him, said, "Why was this fragrant oil
> not sold for three hundred denarii and given to the
> poor?" This he said, not that he cared for the poor,
> but because he was a thief, and had the money box;
> and he used to take what was put in it. But Jesus said,
> "Let her alone; she has kept this for the day of My
> burial. For the poor you have with you always, but
> Me you do not have always." (John 12:1–8)

Mary didn't care what those who were there that day
thought of her. Her love for Jesus had greatly deepened—
when she understood why he didn't respond to her request
to heal her brother. He did abundantly above all that she
could have asked. He raised Lazarus from the dead! And
then Jesus honored her beloved sibling by having him sit at
the table with him.

She therefore honored Jesus in a pure act of worship. She anointed his lowly feet with her precious ointment, then she wiped his feet with her hair. The Scriptures tell us a woman's hair is her glory (see 1 Corinthians 11:15). Think of any young woman who sits in front of the mirror and brushes her long and beautiful hair. It shines like gold as it reflects the early morning sun. To her, her hair is very precious. But Mary used hers as an old rag to wipe the feet of Jesus. She was giving her highest for his lowest.

Our trials are precious because they take us to a place of realizing that everything we have belongs to God, and a yielded heart will do what Mary did. It will place its most valuable possession at the feet of Jesus in an act of worship:

> The twenty-four elders fall down before Him who sits on the throne and worship Him who lives forever and ever, and cast their crowns before the throne, saying:
> "You are worthy, O Lord,
> To receive glory and honor and power;
> For You created all things,
> And by Your will they exist and were created."
> (Revelation 4:10–11)

We don't value what this world values because we are no longer of this world. Our most precious possessions are worthless compared to Jesus: "Yet indeed I also count all things loss for the excellence of the knowledge of Christ

Jesus my Lord, for whom I have suffered the loss of all things, and count them as rubbish, that I may gain Christ" (Philippians 3:8).

Something very precious came from my dark experience, something that I find very difficult to put into words. I now have a greater love for God and a Grand Canyon of gratitude for salvation that has grown even deeper. There is an inner brokenness—a very real humility of heart—and a joyful but helpless dependence on the lover of my soul. I have more empathy for those who are sick and in pain. I cry more easily, I pray more earnestly for those who are destined for the agonies of hell, and I plead with more passion for the lost to trust in Jesus.

While I can see (and appreciate) the value of these virtues, God values them *infinitely* more than I do. He sends a ferocious wind to blow against the tree so that it bends almost double *because* he knows the trauma will send its roots deep into the soil, and the result will be that it will produce more precious fruit.

The moment you put your trust in Jesus, you can have absolute assurance that you are saved (see John 5:24; 1 John 5:11–13). Salvation is a done deal because Jesus finished it all on the cross. Now we need only to hold his hand and trust him, knowing that he promises to never to let us go—in life or in death. Look at Romans 8:38–39:

> For I am persuaded that neither death nor life, nor
> angels nor principalities nor powers, nor things present

nor things to come, nor height nor depth, nor any
other created thing, shall be able to separate us from
the love of God which is in Christ Jesus our Lord.

Neither the trials of life nor death itself can keep
us from the love of God. And never forget that his love
remains steadfast when the sun shines or the storm rages
(see Hebrews 12:3–6). Therefore, do yourself the greatest of
favors—cultivate your faith in Jesus while you face the daily
storms of this life, and when the big one comes, when you
face death, you will be able to face it without fear.

In the next chapter, we will look further at how faith
is the oxygen that keeps us alive when all the air seems to
have been sucked out of the room.

WORDS OF COMFORT

> Casting all your care upon Him,
> for He cares for you.
> (1 Peter 5:7)

Care produces fear. So we must get rid of it quickly. Scripture uses the word *casting*. The process is ongoing. We must *continually* cast our cares upon him so that fear becomes like water that cannot penetrate a duck's back. Anxiety should have no place in the heart of a Christian because it is evidence of a lack of trust in God. "For He *cares* for you." In other words, the love that he proved at the cross is evidenced through his daily care. Believe it and you will have peace. Doubt it and you will have fear. The daily choice is ours.

CHAPTER EIGHT

THE FIGHT FOR FAITH

As we have seen, the Scriptures teach me that if God doesn't run to rescue me from trials, it doesn't mean that he doesn't care. Neither does it mean that he doesn't love me. We saw that in the last chapter. We trust him even if the heavens are silent. In this chapter, we are going to take the issue a little deeper.

Faith brings with it the knowledge that God has a better and higher purpose. I may not understand that higher purpose now, but my trust in his integrity sees what I can't see. It's the evidence of things not seen: "Now faith is the substance of things hoped for, the evidence of things not seen" (Hebrews 11:1).

God didn't remove the children of Israel from the edge of the Red Sea. He led them to it knowing that it was a dead-end street. Then he opened the street. He didn't remove Daniel from the lions' den. He closed the mouths of the lions. He didn't deliver Jesus from the hands of the Romans when they nailed him to the cross. No doubt that those who were eyewitnesses to his suffering desperately prayed that God would intervene:

> Now from the sixth hour until the ninth hour there was darkness over all the land. And about the ninth hour Jesus cried out with a loud voice, saying, "Eli, Eli, lama sabachthani?" that is, "My God, My God, why have You forsaken Me?"
> (Matthew 27:45–46)

Maybe those who stood at the foot of the cross whispered an amen when Jesus cried for help with a loud voice. God had obviously turned his back on Jesus. But those who knew Scripture knew that he had a higher purpose. He had a better plan. Much better. Jesus was fulfilling the words of Scripture:

> My God, My God, why have You forsaken Me?
> Why are You so far from helping Me,
> And from the words of My groaning?
> O My God, I cry in the daytime,
> but You do not hear;
> And in the night season, and am not silent.
> But You are holy,
> Enthroned in the praises of Israel.
> Our fathers trusted in You;

They trusted, and You delivered them.
They cried to You, and were delivered;
They trusted in You, and were not ashamed.
(Psalm 22:1–5)

It was because of that divine plan that the Father turned his holy eyes from the sin that fell on his Son, and he did so because he was delivering those who would trust him from the power of death. He didn't save Jesus because in Jesus he was saving us. When we grasp the "higher purpose" truth, it becomes our anchor in the storm. It means that we can sleep on a pillow in the storm, and that wonderfully soft pillow is the pillow of trust. In speaking of Jesus trusting God in a storm, Charles Spurgeon said,

> He had perfect confidence in God that all was well. The waves might roar, the winds might rage, but He was not at all disquieted by their fury. He knew that the waters were in the hollow of His Father's hand, and that every wind was but the breath of His Father's mouth; and so He was not troubled; nay, He had not even a careful thought, He was as much at ease as on a sunny day. His mind and heart were free from every kind of care, for amid the gathering tempest He deliberately laid Himself down, and slept like a weary child. He went to the hinder part of the ship, most out of the gash of the spray; He took a pillow, and put it under His head, and with fixed intent

disposed Himself to slumber. It was His own act and deed to go to sleep in the storm; He had nothing for which to keep awake, so pure and perfect was His confidence in the great Father. What an example this is to us! We have not half the confidence in God that we ought to have, not even the best of us. The Lord deserves our unbounded belief, our unquestioning confidence, our undisturbed reliance. Oh, that we rendered it to Him as the Saviour did![19]

Look at how high God's purposes are above our own:

"For My thoughts are not your thoughts,
Nor are your ways My ways," says the LORD.
"For as the heavens are higher than the earth,
So are My ways higher than your ways,
And My thoughts than your thoughts."
(Isaiah 55:8–9)

Through faith we see the heaven's perspective rather than that of the earth. The natural eye can only see the Red Sea, the lions' teeth, the horror of the cross, and death as a door closing on life. But the eye that believes (trusts) sees death as an open door. It's not the end. It's the wonderful beginning. Such is the hope we have in Christ.

---

19   C.H. Spurgeon, "Jesus Asleep on a Pillow," Bible Commentary, accessed on September 22, 2020, http://www.asermon.com/books/spurgeon-tilhecome-jesusasleep.html.

The Red Sea was big, cold, wet, and impassible. The lions' teeth were sharp and deadly. Jesus was being cut down by the grim reaper. We don't deny the reality of the problem. We look beyond it. We "stand still, and see the salvation of the LORD" (Exodus 14:13).

Look at how Paul looks to the cross and reaffirms God's love and lists the trials that can come our way—and then note how he tastefully sandwiches it all in divine love:

> What then shall we say to these things? If God is for us, who can be against us? He who did not spare His own Son, but delivered Him up for us all, how shall He not with Him also freely give us all things? Who shall bring a charge against God's elect? It is God who justifies. Who is he who condemns? It is Christ who died, and furthermore is also risen, who is even at the right hand of God, who also makes intercession for us. Who shall separate us from the love of Christ? Shall tribulation, or distress, or persecution, or famine, or nakedness, or peril, or sword? As it is written:
>
> "For Your sake we are killed all day long;
> We are accounted as sheep for the slaughter."
>
> Yet in all these things we are more than conquerors through Him who loved us. For I am persuaded that neither death nor life, nor angels nor principalities nor powers, nor things present nor things to come, nor height nor depth, nor any other created

thing, shall be able to separate us from the love of God which is in Christ Jesus our Lord.
(Romans 8:31–39)

These are the instructions on the back of the hotel door. They are saying, "Don't panic. Stay low. Use the knowledge you have to escape."

We are more than conquerors through him that loved us—even in the face of death. Again, this faithful attitude isn't one of mind over matter but rather faith lifting us above circumstances. It is trusting in the parachute, knowing that it was packed by the most trustworthy of hands and therefore it *cannot* fail. It is knowing the outcome of the game and rejoicing *now* in the victory. We need not stress or stumble as the world does. Remember what Jesus said, "Are there not twelve hours in the day? If anyone walks in the day, he does not stumble, because he sees the light of this world. But if one walks in the night, he stumbles, because the light is not in him" (John 11:9–10).

DOUBTING THOMAS

Through the narrative of John 11, we can learn from Thomas. Jesus tells his disciples of his plans to go to Bethany: "These things He said, and after that He said to them, 'Our friend Lazarus sleeps, but I go that I may wake him up'" (John 11:11). Look at what Thomas then said: "Then Thomas, who is called the Twin, said to his fellow

disciples, 'Let us also go, that we may die with Him'"
(John 11:16).

Jesus had just said that Lazarus was dead. Then he said,
"And I am glad for your sakes that I was not there, that you
may believe. Nevertheless let us go to him" (John 11:15).

Thomas knew that the Jews were seeking to kill Jesus,
and instead of trusting him, he suggested that they go with
him and die. Doubt is certainly depressingly dark and
deeply discouraging. Faith looks for the light. Even when
Jesus rose from the dead *as he said he would*, Thomas didn't
believe—and two thousand years later, his name is synony-
mous with *doubt*:

> Thomas, called the Twin, one of the twelve, was not
> with them when Jesus came. The other disciples
> therefore said to him, "We have seen the Lord."
> So he said to them, "Unless I see in His hands the
> print of the nails, and put my finger into the print of
> the nails, and put my hand into His side, I will not
> believe."
>
> And after eight days His disciples were again
> inside, and Thomas with them. Jesus came, the doors
> being shut, and stood in the midst, and said, "Peace
> to you!" Then He said to Thomas, "Reach your finger
> here, and look at My hands; and reach your hand
> here, and put it into My side. Do not be unbelieving,
> but believing." And Thomas answered and said to
> Him, "My Lord and my God!"

Jesus said to him, "Thomas, because you have seen Me, you have believed. Blessed are those who have not seen and yet have believed." (John 20:24–29)

It's hard to believe that Thomas was so unbelieving because he presumably went with Jesus and had already been an eyewitness as to what had followed this scene of despair and unbelief:

When Jesus came, He found that he had already been in the tomb four days. Now Bethany was near Jerusalem, about two miles away. And many of the Jews had joined the women around Martha and Mary, to comfort them concerning their brother. Then Martha, as soon as she heard that Jesus was coming, went and met Him, but Mary was sitting in the house. (John 11:17–20)

When we believe that a friend has let us down, we have some choices to make. We can break off the friendship and then become resentful and bitter, or we can be quick to forgive. As soon as Martha heard that Jesus was coming, she went to meet him. She valued his friendship and wanted to talk to him about his delay. The Scriptures say, "but Mary was sitting in the house." The "but" is telling. She didn't even want to ask Jesus for an explanation. There couldn't be one. Her beloved brother was dead, and Jesus had shown up late. It was a matter of "too little, too late." Game over.

Sometimes pain casts a very long shadow. And it was in the dark shadow that Mary let her doubts have their way.

But Martha wanted to know *why* he ignored their plea. There *had* to be extenuating circumstances. How could Jesus do nothing when it was in his power to heal her brother?

THE ISSUE OF SUFFERING

We have a similar dilemma with the issue of suffering. How could God do nothing when there is so much suffering throughout this sad world? Children get terrible cancers and die, and God does nothing. Yet we know that he has the power to heal. His no-show would be a terribly disheartening mystery if we were faithless. In the midst of suffering, Giant Despair waits for us to enter Doubting Castle. Its doors seem to welcome us in, as if there is some sort of consolation inside. But there's not. The only comfort in our trials is to trust in the promises of a faithful Creator.

Look at Martha wrestle with the "why" issue, and see how she won the fight by keeping her trust in Jesus:

> Martha said to Jesus, "Lord, if You had been here, my brother would not have died. But even now I know that whatever You ask of God, God will give You." Jesus said to her, "Your brother will rise again." Martha said to Him, "I know that he will rise again in the resurrection at the last day." Jesus said to her, "I am the resurrection and the life. He who believes

in Me, though he may die, he shall live. And whoever lives and believes in Me shall never die. Do you
believe this?" She said to Him, "Yes, Lord, I believe
that You are the Christ, the Son of God, who is to
come into the world." (John 11:21–27)

There was a famous song from the 1960s by Roger
Whitaker called, "I Don't Believe in 'If' Anymore." It spoke
of the word "if" as being an illusion. Martha was appealing
to the "if" with Jesus: "Lord, *if* You had been here..." Here's
the cold reality: he wasn't here. Face reality. Forget it. Move
on. You can't change the past.

But reality isn't over when it comes to God because he
isn't bound by time or natural law. He isn't hindered even
slightly by the "finality" of death. Lazarus was merely sleeping.

When Martha affirmed her trust in Jesus, he told her
that her brother was going to come back to life. He obviously wasn't speaking of her brother coming out of the
grave. That just doesn't happen. She, therefore, thought
that he was making a reference to the final resurrection of
the just and the unjust. Jesus then responded with something that is so profound, few could do it literary justice.
When she said that she knew Lazarus would rise again in
the resurrection at the last day, Jesus said to her, "I am the
resurrection and the life." How unfathomable are those
words! There is not a single atom in a drop of the ocean
that isn't held together by Jesus. Everything is held in his
hand—from the atom in the very center of the sun to the

one in the middle of your eyeball. It did not, does not, will not, and cannot exist without him. He is the life source itself, and he is, therefore, the resurrection power that will awaken the dead.

In speaking of Jesus, Scripture says,

> He is the image of the invisible God, the firstborn over all creation. *For by Him all things were created* that are in heaven and that are on earth, visible and invisible, whether thrones or dominions or principalities or powers. All things were created through Him and for Him. And He is before all things, and in Him all things consist. (Colossians 1:15–17, emphasis added)

This is something different than pantheism—the idea that creation and God are one. It's saying that he is not only the Maker but also the Sustainer of all things:

> Who being the brightness of His glory and the express image of His person, and upholding all things by the word of His power, when He had by Himself purged our sins, sat down at the right hand of the Majesty on high. (Hebrews 1:3)

Look at the translation of this same verse in the Amplified Bible:

> The Son is the radiance and only expression of the glory of [our awesome] God [reflecting God's Shekinah glory, the Light-being, the brilliant light of

the divine], and the exact representation and perfect imprint of His [Father's] essence, and upholding and maintaining and propelling all things [the entire physical and spiritual universe] by His powerful word [carrying the universe along to its predetermined goal]. When He [Himself and no other] had [by offering Himself on the cross as a sacrifice for sin] accomplished purification from sins and established our freedom from guilt, He sat down [revealing His completed work] at the right hand of the Majesty on high [revealing His Divine authority].

Without his power holding it together, every atom in the universe would fall apart. Such thoughts are too high for us. However, such thoughts have the ability to explode our view of God and, in doing so, enlarge our faith. A lack of faith often traces itself back to a lack of knowledge of his power and ability.

Never forget that faith in God is not hard to possess. Do you have faith in a spouse? Is it hard to trust that person? If they love you and you love them, you will trust them no matter what the circumstance. Look at Paul's words of faith that he wrote in the midst of his own trial: "For our light affliction, which is but for a moment, is working for us a far more exceeding and eternal weight of glory" (2 Corinthians 4:17).

Such faith makes Goliath seem small.

MARTHA'S SUBTLE MISTAKE

Dear Martha. She kept strong when Mary didn't. But even though she held her shield high in battle, a subtle but fiery dart made its way to her heart.

It was the prince of preachers, Charles Spurgeon, who said of Martha,

> Martha is a very accurate type of a class of anxious believers. They do believe truly, but not with such confidence as to lay aside their care. They do not distrust the Lord, or question the truth of what He says, yet they puzzle their brain about "How shall this thing be?" and so they miss the major part of the present comfort which the word of the Lord would minister to their hearts if they received it more simply. *How?* and *why?* belong unto the Lord. It is His business to arrange matters so as to fulfil His own promises.[20]

We never need to be anxious because *presently* God is at work in us to will and do his good pleasure. *Right now* Jesus himself as the conqueror of death:

> Inasmuch then as the children have partaken of flesh and blood, He Himself likewise shared in the same, *that through death He might destroy him who had the*

---

20   C. H. Spurgeon, "Though He Were Dead: A Sermon," The Spurgeon Archive, September 14, 1884, https://archive.spurgeon.org/sermons/1799.php.

power of death, that is, the devil, and release those who through fear of death were all their lifetime subject to bondage." (Hebrews 2:14–15, emphasis added)

Satan "had" the power of death. The keys are no longer his: "I am He who lives, and was dead, and behold, I am alive forevermore. Amen. And I have the keys of Hades and of Death" (Revelation 1:18).

He who once danced on our graves fell in.

Martha reminds us of Scripture's admonition to "be anxious for nothing." In other words, nothing should make us anxious. However, we're not simply told to rid ourselves of anxiety. We are told to *replace* it, and the result will be peace:

Be anxious for nothing, but *in everything by prayer and supplication, with thanksgiving, let your requests be made known to God*; and the peace of God, which surpasses all understanding, will guard your hearts and minds through Christ Jesus. (Philippians 4:6–8, emphasis added)

The Most Important Question

Even though Martha was struggling, she knew the right answer to the most important of questions. Jesus asked Martha: "Do you believe this?" She said to him, "Yes, Lord, I believe that You are the Christ, the Son of God, who is to come into the world." Can *you* say that? I hope you can. Salvation is so simple. Trust in Jesus as your Sin-Bearer. He is the resurrection and the life. We're not. That's enough incentive to believe in him.

We are told that Martha went "and secretly called Mary her sister, saying, 'The Teacher has come and is calling for you'" (John 11:28).

Perhaps when Lazarus fell deathly sick, Mary had told her friends that all would be well. She had sent for Jesus, and he wouldn't disappoint her because he not only loved Mary and Martha, but he also loved Lazarus. And now his name was whispered because that most wonderful friendship had left her with the hollow feeling that rejection leaves. Martha knew that, and so she *secretly* called her—not knowing how her sister would react to the news that Jesus had finally arrived. But she need not have been concerned:

> As soon as she heard that, she arose quickly and came to Him. Now Jesus had not come into the town, but was in the place where Martha met Him. Then the Jews who were with her in the house, and comforting her, when they saw that Mary rose up quickly and went out, followed her, saying, "She is going to the tomb to weep there." Then, when Mary came where Jesus was, and saw Him, she fell down at His feet, saying to Him, "Lord, if You had been here, my brother would not have died." (John 11:29–32)

Mary hadn't lost her faith in Jesus. There was no one else like him. She couldn't turn her back on him because he had the words of eternal life. She fell at his feet. That's what we must do in fiery trials. When life hits us with a deadly blow, we don't fall down in despair. We instead fall at the feet of Jesus. We are often broken because of trials, but we're never in despair. He is our only shelter in the storm. While the unbelievers turn to drink or drugs or take their own lives in utter despair, we run to the secret place of the Most High. Look at the apostle Paul speak of being kept in trials:

> We have this treasure in earthen vessels, that the excellence of the power may be of God and not of us. We are hard-pressed on every side, yet not crushed; we are perplexed, but not in despair; per-secuted, but not forsaken; struck down, but not destroyed—always carrying about in the body the dying of the Lord Jesus, that the life of Jesus also may be manifested in our body. For we who live are always delivered to death for Jesus' sake, that the life of Jesus also may be manifested in our mortal flesh. (2 Corinthians 4:7–11)

Mary and Martha were crushed by the loss of their brother, but they kept their eyes on Jesus—and in the next chapter we will stand in awe as he turns their mourning into joy.

WORDS OF COMFORT

> Are not two sparrows sold for a copper coin? And not one of them falls to the ground apart from your Father's will. But the very hairs of your head are all numbered. Do not fear therefore; you are of more value than many sparrows.
>
> (Matthew 10:29–31)

Sparrows are as common as sand. While many other species of birds are remarkable and colorful, sparrows are comparatively dull and look the same the world over. Yet God knows them as individuals and thinks on them.

Our consolation as human beings is that though there are *billions* in the world, no matter how dull we think we are, God knows us by name, knows how many hairs are on our heads, thinks on us, and greatly *values* us. To him, you are of *more* value than *many* sparrows. It is because of his great love that Jesus said, "Do not fear therefore."

CHAPTER NINE

DO NOT MARVEL

We have been looking at the most tragic of human dramas. There had been a death in the family. With all of life's trials, this is one we fear most. Both Mary and Martha were shaken by the death of Lazarus, yet they had hope in Jesus. That hopeful expectation had become a non-event, and as the Scriptures say, "Hope deferred makes the heart sick" (Proverbs 13:12). Heartsick though they were, this wasn't the end of their story.

Through the pages of Holy Scripture, we are going to relive the raising of Lazarus from the dead. The eye of faith will make us eyewitnesses to Jesus' majesty. May the Holy Spirit make it come alive for us. We are going to see a miracle that is a precursor to the final resurrection of billions from their graves.

We would consider the raising of just one four-day-dead man from the grave to be marvelous, but Jesus said *not* to marvel at what he is going to do at the resurrection: "Do not marvel at this; for the hour is coming in which all who are in the graves will hear His voice" (John 5:28).

The reason we shouldn't marvel is because he created the entire universe with his Word. Awakening humanity from the sleep of death with one shout will be a breeze. A piece of plain old cake. As with Lazarus, Scripture refers to death in Christ as a mere sleep. In Jesus, we are not as those who have no hope:

> I do not want you to be ignorant, brethren, concerning those who have fallen asleep, lest you sorrow as others who have no hope. For if we believe that Jesus died and rose again, even so God will bring with Him those who sleep in Jesus. For this we say to you by the word of the Lord, that we who are alive and remain until the coming of the Lord will by no means precede those who are asleep. For the Lord Himself will descend from heaven with a shout, with the voice of an archangel, and with the trumpet of God. And the dead in Christ will rise first. Then we who are alive and remain shall be caught up together with them in the clouds to meet the Lord in the air. And thus we shall always be with the Lord. Therefore comfort one another with these words. (1 Thessalonians 4:13–18)

Do you have comfort in the knowledge that you are saved from the power of death? Do you remember the moment he called your name? Has death lost its terrible sting for you? Has he given you beauty for ashes and the oil of joy for mourning? Is your faith lifting you above your fears? Now, take comfort in what happens as Jesus prepares to wreck this funeral:

> When Jesus saw her weeping, and the Jews who came with her weeping, He groaned in the spirit and was troubled. And He said, "Where have you laid him?"
>
> They said to Him, "Lord, come and see."
>
> Jesus wept. Then the Jews said, "See how He loved him!"
>
> And some of them said, "Could not this Man, who opened the eyes of the blind, also have kept this man from dying?" (John 11:33–37)

Jesus wept. It's the shortest verse in the Bible, yet it stands tall as a giant testament to the great love and compassion he has for you and me. *Compassion* means "to suffer with." Jesus wept with those who mourned. Even though he knew that Lazarus would rise from the dead, he was moved by the power of empathy for their pain. That same empathy should grip the heart of every Christian. Tears should fill our eyes that the thought of the unsaved sitting in the shadow of death, and we should groan in prayer until the power of the gospel takes them from darkness to light.

> Jesus, again groaning in Himself, came to the tomb. It was a cave, and a stone lay against it. Jesus said, "Take away the stone."
>
> Martha, the sister of him who was dead, said to Him, "Lord, by this time there is a stench, for he has been dead four days."
>
> Jesus said to her, "Did I not say to you that if you would believe you would see the glory of God?" Then they took away the stone from the place where the dead man was lying. And Jesus lifted up His eyes and said, "Father, I thank You that You have heard Me. And I know that You always hear Me, but because of the people who are standing by I said this, that they may believe that You sent Me." Now when He had said these things, He cried with a loud voice, "Lazarus, come forth!" And he who had died came out bound hand and foot with graveclothes, and his face was wrapped with a cloth. Jesus said to them, "Loose him, and let him go." (John 11:38–44)

Jesus could have rolled the stone away miraculously. He calmed a storm, spoke to a tree and caused it to wither and die, and multiplied fish and bread. But he didn't move this stone. He instead had his followers remove it. And so almighty God condescends to have us as co-laborers with him in the gospel (see 1 Corinthians 3:9). We will look at this more closely a little later.

Martha stayed in character. As we saw in the previous chapter, she had a measure of faith, but she lacked complete trust. Here, her doubt was revealed by her concern that her brother's body was in decomposition. He was four days dead. The stone should be left in place. No one could help, and nothing could be done for him. That is a reasonable conclusion for someone who lacks faith. But trusting in Jesus opens closed doors. With God *nothing* is impossible. And so Jesus gently rebuked her lack of trust. He reminded her, "Did I not say to you that if you would believe you would see the glory of God?"

Jesus reaffirmed his trust in the Father, then in a loud voice, spoke to a man who was doornail-dead. That very second, his corrupted flesh, his dried blood, and his withered heart responded to the voice of the Son of God—as creation did in the beginning when he said, "Let there be light." The heart of Lazarus answered with one beat and then a second as it began to pump blood. Then his lungs contracted and pulled in air to give oxygen to the blood as it began to flow through his veins. The energy of life gave movement to his limbs.

Can you see movement in the darkness of the open tomb and then see the figure of Lazarus slowly appear out of what was the shadow of death? Can you feel the breathtaking revelation—*that the rising of this one man from the dead actually vindicated that Jesus had ultimate power over the grim reaper?*

Can you see the wide-open mouths of onlookers as they stood in unbelief at what they were seeing? Can you see the tears welling and hear the gasps and cries of the crowd, of what were supposed to be sobbing mourners?

When Lazarus came out of the tomb, his hands, his feet, and his face were bound with graveclothes. He had been brought back from death, but he needed help from those who witnessed the miracle. When Jesus frees us from death, we need other Christians to love and encourage us in our newly resurrected life. I have fond memories of things that were said and done for me in the early days of my walk. It's not a good sign when someone makes a profession of faith but needs no one and nothing but himself. Rather, evidence that we have escaped the power of death will be that we will humbly gravitate toward other Christians: "We know that we have passed from death to life, because we love the brethren. He who does not love his brother abides in death" (1 John 3:14).

If we have passed from death to life, we won't want to stay in our pre-conversion graveclothes. But sins that we once served will still cling our sinful flesh—*especially* the sin of lust, which we will look at in depth in a later chapter.

Lazarus, You, and Me

The believer is a "type" of Lazarus. In Christ, we have been raised from the dead:

> You He made alive, *who were dead in trespasses and sins*, in which you once walked according to the course of this world, according to the prince of the power of the air, the spirit who now works in the sons of disobedience, among whom also we all once conducted ourselves in the lusts of our flesh, fulfilling the desires of the flesh and of the mind, and were by nature children of wrath, just as the others. But God, who is rich in mercy, because of His great love with which He loved us, *even when we were dead in trespasses*, made us alive together with Christ (by grace you have been saved), and raised us up together, and made us sit together in the heavenly places in Christ Jesus, that in the ages to come He might show the exceeding riches of His grace in His kindness toward us in Christ Jesus. (Ephesians 2:1–7, emphasis added)

That night, way back in 1971, Jesus called me from the tomb of darkness into the glorious light. My righteousness deeds were as filthy graveclothes and my sins an offense to the nostrils of a holy God. He has already called me by name, rescued me from death. I therefore have nothing to fear in the face of my passing from this life. All I need do is keep my precious faith in Jesus (see 2 Peter 1:1).

DRIVEN CRAZY

God has done so much for us in Christ. We are not only saved from the terrors of a very real hell, but we are saved from death itself. There are no words to describe what we have in him. Metaphors so often fall short, but I will try to explain the inexplicable.

Have you ever driven into the early morning sun when it's just come over the horizon? It's blinding. It makes you squint. You can't see where you're going, and if your windshield is dirty, it makes seeing clearly even harder.

Have you then driven in the late afternoon with the sun low in the horizon, but this time behind you? There's no squinting. It's not annoying. Everything is very clear. You can see where you're going, and even if your windshield isn't the cleanest, it's no big deal.

Before we are born again, it's like driving into the sun. Nothing is clear. We are not sure of the origin of the universe. We are not clear about when and how life began. Scientists don't know. They are still trying to find out, and so our origin is said to be one of the great mysteries of life. Neither are we clear on the purpose of human existence. What is the meaning of life? That is said to be another great mystery. We don't know. Then there is the greatest mystery.

What happens to us after we die? We haven't a clue. We don't see clearly when it comes to the most frightening of issues.

However, the moment we are come to the Savior, we see all things clearly. No longer do we walk in darkness. These three great mysteries are solved in Christ. Our darkened understanding is enlightened through the light of the gospel. We know our origins. In the beginning, God created the heavens and the earth, and then he made mankind in his image, as male and female. We know the meaning of life. We were made by God for his pleasure and our God-given pleasure. That's the purpose of our existence. And the third and ominous mystery is solved the moment we believe. After we die, the Scriptures say that we go into God's presence. And those who are clean in his sight (through the forgiveness of the cross) enter into his glorious kingdom—where there with be no disease, pain, suffering, or death. Any stains on the windshield of our soul are merely incidental. They don't matter. The moment we turn around and "kiss the Son," he is now for us. Our past, present, and future battle with sin has been dealt with once and for all. If dirt clings to us, we confess our sins, and the Lord is then "faithful and just to forgive us our sins and to cleanse us from all unrighteousness" (1 John 1:9).

WORDS OF COMFORT

Let us run with endurance the race that is set before us, looking unto Jesus, the author and finisher of our faith, who for the joy that was set before Him endured the cross, despising the shame, and has sat down at the right hand of the throne of God. (Hebrews 12:1–2)

"Looking to Jesus" doesn't simply mean to gaze toward the heavens. It means to look to him for your peace, your joy, your salvation, and your every need. Look to him as the focal point of your affections. He is not only the author and finisher of our faith; he's also the author of our lives, the conqueror of death, and the lover of our souls.

CHAPTER TEN

THE BEDFELLOWS

Fear and doubt are bedfellows. As we have seen, they go hand in hand. If I doubt the ability of a parachute to save me, I open the door to fear. Faith closes the door. That's a simple but a profound truth.

However, there is a more subtle dissipater of faith. Instead of doubting the ability of the parachute to save, it comes as a distraction. It whispers, "Put the parachute aside. I have something better. Much better." That's the insidious lie of every temptation to sin.

When we come to Christ, the Bible says that we become partakers of the divine nature:

> …by which have been given to us exceedingly great and precious promises, that through these you may be partakers of the divine nature, having

> escaped the corruption that is in the world
> through lust. (2 Peter 1:4)

God begins to work his will into our lives as we believe in and appropriate his precious promises. Instead of hatred envy and gossip, our lives exhibit love and kindness. We are quick to forgive. We strive to be kind and to do good to others. We not only see what Jesus did through the pages of Scripture, but we also imitate him because the Spirit of Christ dwells in us. We have treasure in earthen vessels—"Christ in you, the hope of glory" (Colossians 1:27)—and his divine nature begins to manifest in us. Having these virtues is the fruit of knowing God.

But there is a big and ugly bug that appears among the fruit—and it will chomp away on the fruit if we let it. It will take away the joy of the Lord and replace it with another joy. It will replace the peace of God with false peace. It will replace our trust in God's promises with doubt. It will replace our security in the promise of heaven with the old, familiar fear of death. This vicious pest is sin.

Some years ago, my daughter gave us a set of very sharp knives as a Christmas gift. I regularly use one that has a serrated edge. It's so sharp that it cuts through almost anything. One day, when that "anything" included my finger, I quickly applied a Band-Aid.

The next morning the skin had done its miracle work, and it was as though I hadn't even been cut. The problem was solved. That is, until I bumped something with my finger and made it bleed again. It took days to completely heal.

I've found that when I think I've overcome what the Bible calls "the flesh"—a particular sin—there's the inevitable bump that causes it to bleed again. I remember thinking how I had finally conquered my appetite problem. The moment I had that thought, the refrigerator called my name, and the beast was let loose with a vengeance.

However, the enemy we fight isn't only the flesh. The real enemy is the demonic realm that inhabits this world. Look at how Scripture puts the crosshairs on this subtle enemy and then zeroes in on our most important defensive weapon:

> Finally, my brethren, be strong in the Lord and in the power of His might. Put on the whole armor of God, that you may be able to stand against the wiles of the devil. For we do not wrestle against flesh and blood, but against principalities, against powers, against the rulers of the darkness of this age, against spiritual hosts of wickedness in the heavenly places. Therefore take up the whole armor of God, that you may be able to withstand in the evil day, and having done all, to stand. Stand therefore, having girded your waist with truth, having put on the breastplate of righteousness, and having shod your feet with the preparation of the gospel of peace; *above all, taking the shield of faith* with which

you will be able to quench all the fiery darts of the
wicked one. (Ephesians 6:10–16, emphasis added)

"Above all, taking the shield of faith." In other words,
we should prioritize faith and take hold of it as a shield. It's
up to us. If we lack faith, fear will rush in like air in a vacuum. In this chapter we are going to look at the importance
of this battle against sin and fear and how to be "strong in
the Lord." To do so, we are going to use the example of a
particularly prevalent sin, one that most of us constantly
battle.

As we've seen, our faith in the Savior is the antidote to
the fear of death. All faith—no fear; all fear—no faith. The
way to strengthen that faith is to draw closer to Jesus, and
the way to destroy it is to give ourselves to sin.

Lust is one attractive sin that loves to call our name.
The moment we think that we are free from its grip, it rears
its ugly head.

The apostle Paul spoke openly about his battle with
lust. It seems almost sacrilegious to say that he had an issue,
but Scripture tells us that those we tend to put on a pedes-
tal of purity were men of like passions. Paul called himself
the chief of sinners, and James said that lust is every man's
problem: "But every man is tempted, when he is drawn
away of his own lust, and enticed" (James 1:14 KJV).

It seems that King Herod was enticed by his own
lust when his eyes fell on the body of a young woman as
she danced (see Mark 6:22), after which she enticed him

further—to commit murder. Many years earlier, another king was similarly enticed by his own lust. This time it was by the sight of a woman as she bathed, and then lust led David by the nose to commit adultery and to also commit murder.

Impaired Judgment

Give yourself to lust and you drive drunk. It will impair your moral judgments so that you cross lines that you normally wouldn't. Lust has brought powerful potentates, politicians, princes, and presidents to public shame.

Lust is a sticky spiderweb, and if we get caught in its grip, it has frightening consequences—in this life and in the next. The hideous spider is always concealed, and its bite is deadly: "Then when lust hath conceived, it bringeth forth sin: and sin, when it is finished, bringeth forth death" (James 1:15 KJV).

Early in Romans chapter 7, after Paul has addressed the subject of adultery, he talks about his personal battle with lust: "I had not known lust, except the law had said, Thou shalt not covet" (Romans 7:7 KJV).

When David coveted his neighbor's wife, that lustful look not only violated the tenth commandment, as we have seen earlier, but it also broke the seventh: "But I say unto you, That whosoever looks on a woman to lust after her hath committed adultery with her already in his heart" (Matthew 5:28 KJV).

NOT A PROBLEM

Before we were regenerated by the Holy Spirit, there was no conflict with lust. Our wandering eyes were full of adultery, and we didn't have an issue with it. Lust was a joyous pleasure, not a plaguing problem. But the moment we turned in genuine repentance, the battle began. The spider came out of hiding the moment it detected a struggle. A man has no problem smoking forty cigarettes a day until he tries to stop. That's when war is declared and the battle begins.

Further on in Romans 7, Paul spoke of this warfare as a clash between two laws: "I see another law in my members, warring against the law of my mind...So then with the mind I myself serve the law of God, but with the flesh the law of sin" (Romans 7:23, 25).

The battle is between the renewed mind and the old sinful flesh. In the following chapter Paul tells us how he found victory: "For the law of the Spirit of life in Christ Jesus has made me free from the law of sin and death" (Romans 8:2).

In Christ Jesus, we are set free from the law of sin and death. We are no longer caught in the web. The suffering of Jesus satisfied the law's demands. The debt had been fully paid. The law no longer legally condemned us (see Romans 8:1). The judge could now smile with pleasure, whereas he once frowned in wrath. Whom the Son set free is free indeed.

Those Uninvited Thoughts

But how can we live in this freedom when uninvited filthy thoughts continue to invade our renewed minds? They promise an unlawful and devilish joy, and their presence steals the joy of the Lord that comes with a pure conscience.

The answer is to build a resistance using something this world despises—the fear of God.

Jesus said three breathtakingly profound words in Luke 8:17. He said, "Nothing is secret." As we saw in a previous chapter, King Solomon came to this same sobering conclusion. "For God shall bring every work into judgment, with every secret thing, whether it be good, or whether it be evil" (Ecclesiastes 12:14 KJV). Paul reiterated this in Romans 2:16: "In the day when God shall judge the secrets of men by Jesus Christ according to my gospel" (KJV).

If God is omniscient, then there is nothing secret. Nothing is hidden from his morally pure eyes (see Proverbs 15:3 and Hebrews 4:13). There has never been a secret murder, a secret rape, or a secret adulterous rendezvous. What is done in Vegas is said to stay in Vegas, but we know that it's also known in heaven. No lustful thought has ever been welcomed that hasn't also been seen by the eyes of God.

It's common to hear the argument that men should refrain from pornography because it's not good for a marriage. The argument is that if you're going to be longingly looking at unattainable women, it's not going to be long until you become tired of your spouse. As we saw earlier, a pornography habit can destroy the excitement and the intimacy of a marriage.

However, the benefits or damages are a side issue. It's like saying that a man should avoid adultery because it's not good for his marriage. Whether it's good or bad isn't the *primary* issue. The issue is that adultery is morally wrong and that it's a sin against God. Pornography is primarily a sin in his eyes, and that's what should be our most sobering concern—not just because it offends him but because of the consequences. A criminal may anger the judge because of his crime. But his *real* concern is a forty-year prison term.

It is evident from his words that Paul feared God, and that was his victory over lust. He said, "Walk in the Spirit, and you will not fulfill the lusts of the flesh" (Galatians 5:16).

NO MATTER HOW THIRSTY

The flesh is a poisoned well. Don't drink from it—no matter how thirsty you feel. If we have a healthy fear of God, even though we have temptations, we will not fulfill the desires of the flesh. Instead, we will turn away, shut our eyes, spit out the poison, cry out to God, or run like Joseph when lust called his name (see Genesis 39:7). And if we do fall into the poisonous well, we will quickly get up and get out, confess our sins, and determine afresh to walk in holiness (see 1 John 1:9).

Yet with all this talk of the lust of the eyes, they're not the cause of the problem. They are just the doorway. Our real problem is what's behind the door. It's our sinful heart. The eyes simply feed the imagination. They provide the spark for the tinder-dry forest. That's why Scripture says to "Keep your heart with all diligence, for out of it spring the issues of life" (Proverbs 4:23). We must do that because we are dealing with issues of life and death. *Our* life and death. Therefore, we must never fall into the subtle trap of thinking that God is somehow sympathetic to our sin. It's clear from what Jesus said that he's not: "And fear not them which kill the body, but are not able to kill the soul: but rather fear him which is able to destroy both soul and body in hell" (Matthew 10:28 KJV).

God is sympathetic to our weaknesses (see Hebrews 4:15) but not to our sin. He forbids only that which will kill us, and he has made a way for us to escape the spider's grip:

> No temptation has overtaken you except such as is common to man; but God is faithful, who will not allow you to be tempted beyond what you are able, but with the temptation will also make the way of escape, that you may be able to bear it. (1 Corinthians 10:13)

The virtue of the fear of God (coupled with a tender conscience) will always look for that way of escape.

OUR CONSOLATION

It is humbling to come back again and again, asking for forgiveness, but keep in mind that whenever we do that sincerely, as far as God is concerned, it's the first time we ever came. Whenever he forgives, God forgets. We have his promise on it: "For I will be merciful to their unrighteousness, and their sins and their iniquities will I remember no more" (Hebrews 8:12 KJV).

There are two great consolations in this ongoing battle we have with lust. The first is that it continually brings us to our knees. And that's the safest place for any Christian. It ensures our dependence on God.

And the second consolation comes in the fact that immediately after talking about the fear of God, Jesus said:

> Are not two sparrows sold for a farthing? and one of them shall not fall on the ground without your Father. But the very hairs of your head are all numbered. Fear ye not therefore, ye are of more value than many sparrows. (Matthew 10:29–31 KJV)

Fear and love are compatible. We can both tremble in fear of God and, at the same time, bask in the knowledge that he loves us. That was evidenced at the cross (see Romans 5:8). And it is because of this great love that he has made provision for those many sins that so easily beset us. In Christ we have escaped the corruption that is in the world through lust. We are free from the deadly spider. So believe his Word by trusting in his exceedingly great and precious promises:

> His divine power has given to us all things that pertain to life and godliness, through the knowledge of Him who called us by glory and virtue, by which have been given to us exceedingly great and precious promises, that through these you may be partakers of the divine nature, having escaped the corruption that is in the world through lust. (2 Peter 1:3–4)

CUSTER'S LUST STAND

One last thing may be helpful in this never-ending battle against the fiery arrows of the enemy. My son-in-law and the president of Living Waters, Emeal (E.Z.) Zwayne, came up with a really good acronym that works when we are tempted by lust. It is "NOPE." NOPE stands for "Not One Peek Even." If I say "NOPE" out loud when Potiphar's wife beckons, I am in essence saying, "NOPE. Not even one little curious look. Not a glance. This is not negotiable. I'm not going there."

It's saying no to the world, to the flesh, and to the devil. In making that bold proclamation, I'm telling demons to get off my shoulder. I don't want their dirty whispers. I'm saying (as Jesus did when he was tempted), "Get behind me, Satan." I'm following Jesus not the devil. So he belongs in my rearview mirror. I'm done with listening to the Father of

Lies. And I'm resisting the devil in the light of the sacrifice of the cross. Why would I yield to the power of lust when it comes as a bedfellow with death and damnation?

This continuing conflict isn't just a battle against my sinful nature:

> We wrestle not against flesh and blood, but against principalities, against powers, against the rulers of the darkness of this world, against spiritual wickedness in high places. Wherefore take unto you the whole armour of God, that ye may be able to withstand in the evil day, and having done all, to stand. (Ephesians 6:12–13 KJV)

We are told to "stand" and can therefore learn a lesson from General Custer. He lost his stand because he underestimated his enemy:

> In less than an hour, the Indians had won the Battle of the Little Bighorn, massacring Custer and every one of his men. The battle has been ennobled as "Custer's Last Stand"—but in truth, Custer and his men never stood a fighting chance…In the end, Custer found himself on the defensive with nowhere to hide and nowhere to run and was killed along with every man in his battalion. His body was found near Custer Hill, also known as Last Stand Hill, alongside the bodies of 40 of his men, including his brother and nephew, and dozens of dead horses.

Custer had suffered two bullet wounds, one near his heart and one in the head. It's unclear which wound killed him or if the head wound happened before or after he died. In the heat of battle, it's unlikely the Indian who shot Custer knew he'd just killed a U.S. Army icon. Even so, once word spread that Custer was dead, many Native Americans claimed to be his executioner.

After the battle, Indians stripped, scalped and dismembered their enemy's corpses on the battlefield, possibly because they believed the souls of disfigured bodies were doomed to walk the earth forever.[21]

Don't Let it Build

While we have looked at lust and seen how it is a powerful and devasting sin, *all* sin should be feared. And fear (when it comes to sin) is appropriate. Any soldier who doesn't fear his enemy has already lost the battle. Fear makes him check his weapons. Fear of being shot through the head makes him secure his helmet. It causes him to *diligently* listen to his instructors. He doesn't want to be in the heat of battle without ammunition or not knowing what he should do next. This fear doesn't make him tremble. It makes him vigilant.

---

21   Annette McDermott, "What Really Happened at the Battle of the Little Bighorn?," History.com, updated June 7, 2019, https://www.history.com/news/little-bighorn-battle-facts-causes.

Fear lying, irrespective of its so-called size or supposed color. Fear theft, irrespective of the value of that which is stolen. Tremble at the very thought of blasphemy coming out of your mouth. Fear gossip, not keeping your word, or greed. And fear transgressing your conscience. Keep it tender, or you will not be able to hear its voice.

Such fears cause us to diligently apply the words of the instructor's Book—that precious lamp to our feet and light to our path.

As lowly human beings—from kings to peasants and from rich men to paupers—we (along with the entire animal kingdom) have to regularly remove poisons from our bodies. This is not a pleasant experience, but it is a most necessary part of healthy living. One way we can tastefully refer to this part of life is to say that we are "relieving" ourselves. Failure to relieve ourselves can be fatal.

So it is with the poison of unconfessed sin. Don't let it build up. Relieve yourself of the burden of sin because it will steal your energy and eventually your spiritual health.

If you fall into some sin through lust or anger or a secret bitterness, don't wait. Rid yourself of it. The Scriptures warn, "He who covers his sins will not prosper, But whoever confesses and forsakes them will have mercy" (Proverbs 28:13).

In March of 1989, Flight 1363 departed from Thunder Bay to Winnipeg on a brutally cold and snowy day. The plane was overweight because extra passengers were aboard from a flight that had been cancelled, forcing the pilot to offload fuel. This meant a stopover in Dryden to refuel would be necessary.

Already running behind schedule and dealing with electrical issues that would have delayed him even more if he shut the plane off, the pilot opted to take the risk of refueling with one engine running. This also meant de-icing the plane would be impossible since doing so with the plane running would allow deadly fumes from the anti-freeze to enter the cabin. Unfortunately, the pilot was unfamiliar with the type of plane he was operating, a Fokker F28, which can lose serious amounts of lift if the wings have even a millimeter of ice.

With a full tank of fuel, the pilot took off, but the plane refused to gain altitude. It began to roll from side to side as it left the runway and glided over the valley beyond. Within forty-nine seconds, the plane and its sixty-five passengers dove into the trees. The plane broke into pieces and burst into flames. Twenty-four passengers and three crew members died in the crash, and many others suffered horrible injuries, including burns from the fire. Ten extra minutes on the runway and the right kind of de-icing fluid may have caused a very different outcome.[22]

---

22   Admiral Cloudberg, "The crashes of Air Ontario flight 1363 and USAir flight 405," Admiral Cloudberg (blog), August 4, 2019, https://admiralcloudberg.medium.com/ the-crashes-of-air-ontario-flight-1363-and-usair-flight-405-357ceee1867.

There is a de-icing that is effective for the Christian. It will stop us from becoming cold in our love for God. It is simply to see our sin in its true light under the spirituality of God's law. That will show us that our Creator is just and good and right to damn us in hell for our sins. That knowledge will produce the long-lasting de-icing fluid of gratitude. It has worked for me for nearly fifty years.

There hasn't been one moment that I've become cold in my love for my God. If that sounds like a proud boast, let me show you why it's not. I have been married to my wonderful wife for the same period of time, and there hasn't been one moment where I have become cold in my love for her. If I had become cold, I would be dishonoring and insulting her. I vowed to love her in good times and in bad, and I haven't wavered because she's easy to love.

Under the light of God's unwavering love for us, it's easy for us to love him. He invaded this evil earth to save us from sin. And sin always comes with its hand in the hand of the grim reaper. Our salvation came with a cost that can never be fully realized this side of heaven. How could we ever become cold in the light of such love? Never. Shame on me if I do.

WORDS OF COMFORT

Yea, though I walk through the valley of the shadow
of death,
I will fear no evil;
For You are with me;
Your rod and Your staff, they comfort me.
(Psalm 23:4)

Sheep are not intelligent creatures. If they stray from the
flock, they are easily lost and easy prey for predators. But
they are safe when taken care of by any good shepherd.
David risked his life for his sheep, but the Son of David gave
his life for his sheep. David fought off a bear and a lion (see
1 Samuel 17:36). Jesus conquered him who had the power
of death. Now we belong to him: "For you were like sheep
going astray, but have now returned to the Shepherd and
Overseer of your souls" (1 Peter 2:25). Now we fear no evil.
In this life or in the next.

CHAPTER ELEVEN

A LIGHTHOUSE

We have looked at what the Bible calls "exceedingly great and precious promises" from the Word of God. While it's the world's most loved publication, it's also the most hated. It's adored by those who obey its precepts and detested by those who don't. It promises peace in troubled times and offers absolute assurance of salvation from death.

My hope is that you believe that and that your faith in Jesus continually overcomes your fear of death. But that hope goes further. I hope you have been so transformed by the power of God that you want to become a lighthouse for those who are still in this dark and stormy world.

In the Scriptures, those who loved God showed their love horizontally. They loved their fellow human beings enough to overcome their own fears and share the gospel. As a new Christian, my first thought was for the salvation of my precious family. If they died in their sins, they would be damned (see Mark 16:16). That horrified me and gave me an earnest desire to find out how I could effectively reach them with the gospel. I hope you're having similar thoughts.

Listen to the apostle Paul give his testimony and watch for where these verses mention you and me:

> And I thank Christ Jesus our Lord who has enabled me, because He counted me faithful, putting me into the ministry, although I was formerly a blasphemer, a persecutor, and an insolent man; but I obtained mercy because I did it ignorantly in unbelief. And the grace of our Lord was exceedingly abundant, with faith and love which are in Christ Jesus. This is a faithful saying and worthy of all acceptance, that Christ Jesus came into the world to save sinners, of whom I am chief. However, for this reason I obtained mercy, that in me first Jesus Christ might show all longsuffering, *as a pattern to those who are going to believe on Him for everlasting life*. Now to the King eternal, immortal, invisible, to God who alone is wise, be honor and glory forever and ever. Amen. (1 Timothy 1:12–17, emphasis added)

Before the apostle Paul came to faith, he was a blasphemer and a persecutor (see Acts 26:11). As Saul of Tarsus, he created havoc within the church by persecuting anyone who named the name of Jesus. But on the road to Damascus, he was stopped in his tracks when Jesus appeared to him from the heavens. Then God *enabled* him because the Lord counted him "faithful." I may not be able to sing and dance or speak with eloquence, and I may not be intelligent, strong, tall, and good looking, but I *can* be faithful. *Anyone* can. Faithfulness is an open book in which we can write our own story.

GOOD ADVICE

Someone once said, "Always eat when you're hungry, always drink when you're dry. Always sleep when you're sleepy, but don't stop breathing or you'll die." That's good advice. But it's misdirected. We are not the ones who determine whether we keep breathing. We draw in breath around twenty thousand times a day with an amazing seven million breathes each year. All this is done with very little help from us. Our life is dependent on whether our lungs work, and yet they function independently of our will. We have no say in the matter. And it's the same case when it comes to our heart, liver, pancreas, and kidneys. So much of life is dependent on that over which we have no control.

But faith in God is different. It's ours to exercise. It is a ball that God has placed in our court. Make it your concerted aim to hit it out of the ballpark. Hebrews chapter 11 is referred to as the "faith" chapter—the Hall of Faith, listing those who broke from convention and completely trusted God. This one chapter in Hebrews uses the word *faith* twenty times. Here is a portion that showcases the accomplishments of those who saw this wonderful truth:

> By faith the walls of Jericho fell down after they were encircled for seven days. By faith the harlot Rahab did not perish with those who did not believe, when she had received the spies with peace. And what more shall I say? For the time would fail me to tell of Gideon and Barak and Samson and Jephthah, also of David and Samuel and the prophets: who through faith subdued kingdoms, worked righteousness, obtained promises, stopped the mouths of lions, quenched the violence of fire, escaped the edge of the sword, out of weakness were made strong, became valiant in battle, turned to fight the armies of the aliens. Women received their dead raised to life again. Others were tortured, not accepting deliverance, that they might obtain a better resurrection. Still others had trial of mockings and scourgings, yes, and of chains and imprisonment. They were stoned, they were sawn in two, were tempted, were slain with the sword. They wandered about in sheepskins and goatskins, being destitute, afflicted, tormented—of whom the world was not worthy. They wandered in deserts and mountains, in dens and caves of the earth.

And all these, having obtained a good testimony through faith, did not receive the promise, God having provided something better for us, that they should not be made perfect apart from us. (Hebrews 11:30–40)

Don't be a Thomas. Trust your Lord. Break free from mediocrity and add your name to the Hall of Faith. Trust the Lord with all your heart. Plead with him to use you. Pray that he gives you wisdom so that you'll know how to share the gospel effectively with the unsaved. Be a lighthouse in this frightening storm of life. The job of lighthouse keepers in past years hasn't been an easy one. They no doubt fought loneliness in the dark hours of the night. But they had to be vigilant. If they slept during a storm or allowed their lights to go out, precious human beings could have been dashed on rocks or sunk into a watery grave. They had to have faith that no matter how great the storm, they were founded on a sure foundation. They had to keep their minds on their moral responsibility to guide those who were caught in the storm.

In the next chapter we will look at some of the conflicts that lie ahead for those who step up for this noble task.

Words of Comfort

> Do not fear, little flock, for it is your Father's good
> pleasure to give you the kingdom.
> (Luke 12:32)

How tender Jesus is toward those who trust in him. The
Good Shepherd knows our battle with fear and tells us why
we should deny it. It is because God is our loving "Abba
Father." And like every loving father, he delights to give to
his children. Every good thing and every seemingly bad
thing come only by his permissive will. He chastens those
he loves. While no chastening is pleasurable, it works for us,
not against us, and that knowledge helps us endure the pain
of life's many trials.

CHAPTER TWELVE

THE AMAZING POWER OF CONFLICT

Conflict is an essential ingredient in every good movie script, in the storyline of a gripping TV program, and in all best-selling novels. If it gets a thumbs up from the public, you can be sure it contains conflict.

Here are two scenarios:

1. A husband comes home and asks how his wife's day went. She says she had a great day. He says that he did as well.

That "story" is dead in the water. It's boring.

2. A husband comes home and asks how his wife's day went. She joyfully breaks the news to him that she found out from the doctor that she is pregnant with

twins! His facial expression turns to dismay as he says, "Oh no! I was fired today!"

Suddenly you have a story. How did she react to his job loss? Why did he get fired? How will they cope? The storyline has drawn you in.

If you watch popular TV programs about couples seeking to purchase a house, you will see conflict in every program. The couple are pitted against each other. In one episode, she may be very opinionated, and she disagrees with his desire to get a house that has a "man cave." The one he likes is obviously the best of the three homes they have seen, but she complains that it's out of their price range. He rolls his eyes as she says that it's not going to happen. There's the conflict. The woman comes across as unreasonable. And so you side with the nice hen-pecked husband.

As the program draws to a close, there's a wonderful twist. The woman changes her mind, puts her loving arms around her husband, and says that he can have his man cave. That gives you the warm fuzzies. And she turned out to be a sweetie. The villain became the hero. You enjoyed the program and will look for others in the series. Multiply that reaction a million times over, and the ratings lift, which in turn sells advertising, and that puts money in the program producer's pocket.

You will even find this same principle in food programs where chefs are pitted against each other, in action movies where the hero overcomes the villain, or in classic movies, such as Ben-Hur, where there is conflict between Ben-Hur and his corrupted boyhood friend, Messala.

Here now is my point: we can use the storytelling wisdom of screenwriters to tell the greatest story of all, the goodness of our deliverance from sin and death through Jesus' work. As discussed in the last chapter, we have the privilege to be lighthouses to warn of danger and light the way to safety. And one way we can do so is by applying the power of conflict. Our YouTube channel has over a hundred million views, and because of its further potential to reach the lost, we have become earnest as to how we present each video. For years we didn't give too much thought to titles. We simply called them whatever came to mind. But when we began to add conflict (with integrity, of course—never promising in the title something that wasn't delivered in the video), we saw something wonderful happen. For example, in one recent open-air preaching clip, I spoke to a young lady who was flippant about the gospel. But when I reasoned with her about something specific, her demeanor completely changed, and she listened intently.

The clip could have been titled "Girl listens to the gospel." Instead, conflict was added when it was titled "She laughs at first...then the preacher says *this*."

That clearly caused questions to be asked: What was it the "this" the preacher said? How did it change her? And the title exploded the viewership to over a million views very quickly. This is important because we're not producing funny cat videos or clips that show death-defying feats. Our videos are a little more important. They tell dying sinners that Jesus Christ conquered death and brought life and immortality to light through the gospel.

Jesus and Conflict

But while a certain amount of conflict can help make our message compelling, we will face actual conflict too as we share the good news with others. In fact, the first sermon Jesus ever preached didn't exactly have the front pews holding up ten-points signs. He didn't even get a thumbs up from the chief rabbi. Instead, he got a unified thumbs down. Roman gladiator thumbs down. They tried to kill him by tossing him off the local cliff.

So what was lacking in his sermon? Was it boring? Was it too long? Did he fail to keep the congregation awake with a touch of humor, or wasn't he able to reach their felt needs?

Let's see where Jesus went wrong:

> So He came to Nazareth, where He had been brought up. And as His custom was, He went into the synagogue on the Sabbath day, and stood up to read. And He was handed the book of the prophet Isaiah. And when He had opened the book, He found the place where it was written:
>
> "The Spirit of the LORD is upon Me,
> Because He has anointed Me

To preach the gospel to the poor;
He has sent Me to heal the brokenhearted,
To proclaim liberty to the captives
And recovery of sight to the blind,
To set at liberty those who are oppressed;
To proclaim the acceptable year of the LORD."

Then He closed the book, and gave it back to the attendant and sat down. And the eyes of all who were in the synagogue were fixed on Him. And He began to say to them, "Today this Scripture is fulfilled in your hearing." So all bore witness to Him, and marveled at the gracious words which proceeded out of His mouth. And they said, "Is this not Joseph's son?"

He said to them, "You will surely say this proverb to Me, 'Physician, heal yourself! Whatever we have heard done in Capernaum, do also here in Your country.'" Then He said, "Assuredly, I say to you, no prophet is accepted in his own country. But I tell you truly, many widows were in Israel in the days of Elijah, when the heaven was shut up three years and six months, and there was a great famine throughout all the land; but to none of them was Elijah sent except to Zarephath, in the region of Sidon, to a woman who was a widow. And many lepers were in Israel in the time of Elisha the prophet, and none of them was cleansed except Naaman the Syrian."

> So all those in the synagogue, when they heard
> these things, were filled with wrath, and rose up and
> thrust Him out of the city; and they led Him to the
> brow of the hill on which their city was built, that
> they might throw Him down over the cliff. Then
> passing through the midst of them, He went His way.
> (Luke 4:16–30)

Aha. There was the problem. He quoted a Messianic prophecy and related it to himself. That will always cause conflict. But that's what Jesus did, wherever he went. The Scriptures tell us that after he spoke, "So there was a division among the people because of Him" (John 7:43). His hearers split in two. When unbelievers ask for evidence that Jesus was who he said he was, some become believers when they are convinced and some don't. As we saw in chapter 6 with the Hollywood stars, people don't see the need for Jesus' message because their pride won't let them admit they need saving. Or more accurately, as John's discussion with me made clear, people don't want evidence because they want to continue in the pleasures of sin.

It even happened when Jesus raised Lazarus from the dead. The incident showed the unbelieving Jews once and for all that this was the promised Messiah. All the rumors about him were true. He could raise the dead:

> Then many of the Jews who had come to Mary, and
> had seen the things Jesus did, believed in Him. But

some of them went away to the Pharisees and told them the things Jesus did. Then the chief priests and the Pharisees gathered a council and said, "What shall we do? For this Man works many signs. If we let Him alone like this, everyone will believe in Him, and the Romans will come and take away both our place and nation." And one of them, Caiaphas, being high priest that year, said to them, "You know nothing at all, nor do you consider that it is expedient for us that one man should die for the people, and not that the whole nation should perish." Now this he did not say on his own authority; but being high priest that year he prophesied that Jesus would die for the nation, and not for that nation only, but also that He would gather together in one the children of God who were scattered abroad. Then, from that day on, they plotted to put Him to death. Therefore Jesus no longer walked openly among the Jews, but went from there into the country near the wilderness, to a city called Ephraim, and there remained with His disciples. (John 11:45–54)

They saw him raise a man from the dead, and yet "from that day on, they plotted to put him to death." This was because the proud religious leaders hated God without cause, and when the Son of God spoke, they hated him also.

And they will hate *us* as well because we belong to him. But being hated is part of this life. People resent other people's politics, their outrageous clothes, weird hairstyles, or the way they talk or live. They are jealous of each other and will gossip at the drop of a hat. The only time they speak well of one another is at a funeral. The nasty, greedy, womanizer becomes a saint in his obituary. But we were saved out of that world: "For we ourselves were also once foolish, disobedient, deceived, serving various lusts and pleasures, living in malice and envy, hateful and hating one another" (Titus 3:3).

It shouldn't surprise us when a nasty world directs its hatred at us. But the conflict that comes our way because we are Christians comes for the most noble of causes. That's why we should rejoice when sinners look down on us as the scum of the earth: "We have been made as the filth of the world, the offscouring of all things until now" (1 Corinthians 4:13).

We are in the best of company. Love this world, pray for them because you love them, and speak the truth in love because you want to see them in heaven not in hell.

WORDS OF COMFORT

Oh, how great is Your goodness,
Which You have laid up for those who fear You,
Which You have prepared for those who trust in You
In the presence of the sons of men!
(Psalm 31:19)

Not too many things in this life deserve an "Oh!" The birth of a child, a spectacular sunrise, or a hummingbird in flight perhaps do. But what God has prepared for those who love and trust him certainly does. Look at 1 Corinthians 2:9:

But as it is written:
"Eye has not seen, nor ear heard,
Nor have entered into the heart of man
The things which God has prepared for those who love Him."

The Old Testament uses the words *fear* and *trust*, while the New Testament uses *love*. If we love God, we will both fear and trust him.

CHAPTER THIRTEEN

THE EVOLUTION OF JERKS

I pulled up to a set of traffic lights in my car and waited as an elderly gentleman cautiously pulled out from his driveway in front of me. As I sat behind his angled vehicle, I quietly said, "No problem, sir. You take your time. It's okay." I wasn't being sarcastic. I was countering an impatience that I detected in myself a week or so earlier when a similar incident took place. It was then that I began to realize that I was being unconsciously manipulated by modern technology.

Years ago, I enjoyed opening credits for movies. Some took one or two minutes to set the scene for the waiting audience. The movie would inform them of the name of the producer, the director, the main actors (in alphabetical order), the type of color in which it was filmed, the quality of sound, and other details. But nowadays, if the opening credits aren't over within about five seconds, I feel an impatience welling in my heart. That's because almost everything has become instantaneous. Products come to the door at lightning speed. It takes me seconds to call my sister seven thousand miles away, and then I see video of her on my phone that comes to me at the speed of light. Literally.

Before the internet, if I wanted specific information to quote in a new book, I would drive to a library and search through their many publications until I found the information for which I was looking. Then I would photocopy it, take it home, and physically type it on a typewriter into my book. Nowadays, it takes me less than one minute to locate the same information online. Books that would have taken me four months to write I can now write in four weeks, if I push myself.

You may have seen a video that went viral of someone that most people identified as a real jerk. He sat in a plane thumping the back of the seat in front of him because the woman passenger had reclined and left him in a cramped space. She had filmed him annoying her and was threatening to take him to court for assault.

Most of us are unconsciously becoming jerks. We are becoming impatient, graceless, *annoying* jerks. There are short fuses in the home between husbands and wives, in the workplace, in the police force, and in the government among politicians. And there's no way we are going to lighten up while technology is winding us up. It's getting worse, and there's no going back. This impatience is resulting in road-rage deaths and in shootings by people who were fired.

But when someone comes to genuine faith in Jesus, there is a positive spinoff. That spinoff is the fruit of the Spirit. Love is patient and kind. It overpowers impatience and lets the elderly man in the car take his time. Love doesn't even think of banging the back of a reclined seat. Neither does it take people to court for frivolous reasons. Husbands who love their wives as Christ loved the church listen to them patiently. Employees who are fired move on without bitterness. When God's love takes rule in a nation, crime is down. So the police officer smiles because he knows he will get home to see his family that night.

And when we are hated because we belong to God, the love of Christ in us will whisper, *Father, forgive them for they do not know what they do* (Luke 23:34).

The End Goal

Babies think they are the center of the universe. From the moment they are born they scream for attention. Their cry is their way of saying, "Feed me or I will die!" So we run to meet their needs. As they grow, we prepare them for life by teaching them the importance of using their manners. *Please* becomes part of their "feed me" vocabulary. Next, we show them how to feed themselves. This is because the goal is to have them stand on their own two feet and then to eventually reproduce of their own kind (within the bounds of marriage, of course).

When we are born again, it seems that God responds to our every demand. Prayers are miraculously answered. But then he steps back to teach us to stand on our own two feet. That's not so much fun because we tend to get bruised as we learn to walk.

The goal is for us to be fruitful and multiply—to reproduce of our own kind. The problem is that many of us are stuck in self-centered infancy. We've learned to walk in Christ and feed ourselves on the Word, but we don't reproduce. We are fearful when it comes to planting the seed of the Word of God in the hearts of the lost. We avoid the very thought of the dreadful task of evangelism.

Arguably, the biggest barrier to the joy of reproduction is fear of rejection. Like a terrified and tongue-tied teenager standing in a dark corner unable to even approach the girl he admires, we are paralyzed by our fears. The spirit is willing, but the flesh is petrified. There is the fear of not knowing what to say...of not being able to answer some tough question. Or the fear of looking foolish. And those fears combine to make a measly molehill look like a massive mountain of intimidation.

I have been witnessing for nearly fifty years, in planes, on buses, in taxis, in airports, in colleges, on the streets, in stores, in season, and out of season. You name it, and I've done it. Yes, even in a public restroom. Despite this glowing and bold testimony, my dark little secret is that I battle fear every time I approach someone. *Everyone* scares me. Zacchaeus never fails to look like a Goliath. God is my witness that when I'm on a plane with an empty seat next to me, I'm praying for the prospective person. I'm secretly praying that they won't show up! I'm serious. But when they do sit in the hot seat, I never fail to witness to them. This is because I have found that there are certain powerful weapons that easily defeat the enemy. Goliath can be taken down with a smooth stone and then taken out completely with his sword.

Spiritual infancy should have been left behind as we grew in Christ. It should have been defeated when we had our Gethsemane experience. As a new Christian, I came to terms with my fears. As I wrestled with the fear of rejection, I sweat drops of blood at the thought of speaking to strangers. My prayer moved from, *Anyone but me*, to *Not my will, but yours be done...send me.* Then I stood to my feet, knowing that the issue of fear was no longer negotiable. Any listening to its further whispering was out of the question—because the fear was rooted in pride and the desire to be accepted by this sinful world. I no longer needed that.

Instead, I would with humility and honor carry the cross and begin to do what I'd been saved to do—to follow Jesus, to seek and save the lost. I would forever pour contempt on my pride. All that happened in a moment of time, in the light of the blood of the cross.

THE OPIATE OF THE MASSES

It was early one Saturday morning, and I was taking my dog for a run on my bike. During the week he sat on a platform, but on Saturdays and Sundays he ran to get some exercise. It was good for him, and he loved it. Someone saw a video I made where he was attached to the bike using a leash and had suggested a special stainless-steel pipe with a spring coil inside. This attached to the bike and to the dog's collar and gave leeway as he ran.

I became accustomed to seeing people smiling as we rode passed because Sam looked very cool as he ran. But one day a man stopped me not knowing that the pipe contained a spring. He was furious because he thought that I was *dragging* my poor dog against his will. I wanted to say that Sam loved running beside the bike, but he wouldn't let me get a word in. As far as he was concerned, I was guilty of animal cruelty, and he was doing the right thing by abusing me. He was so angry that I felt that my life was in danger.

So it is with the godless world. To them, Christianity is the opiate of the masses. If we want to go to heaven, we are forced to follow strict religious rules. We are dragged along by fear and that makes them feel justifiably indignant.

What they don't know is that we are willingly yoked to Jesus. His yoke is easy, and his burden is light (see Matthew 11:29–30). We *delight* to do his will. We don't have to drag ourselves to do what pleases him—because he has given us a new heart and caused us to joyfully walk in his statutes.

While I (like every Christian) have a battle with my two natures—when my spirit is willing but my flesh is weak—I daily deny myself the pleasures of sin, take up my cross, and follow Jesus. But I do this willingly. Love gives me the energy to run to do his will. I gladly read my Bible because it is full of exceedingly great and precious promises. It's a bright lamp to my feet and a light to my path. I gladly share my faith because it's the right thing to do.

Look at how Scripture speaks to the world's misunderstandings of why we live godly:

> Therefore, since Christ suffered in the flesh [and died for us], arm yourselves [like warriors] with the same purpose [being willing to suffer for doing what is right and pleasing God], because whoever has suffered in the flesh [being like-minded with Christ] is done with [intentional] sin [having stopped pleasing the world], so that he can no longer spend the rest of his natural life living for human appetites and desires, but [lives] for the will and purpose of God. For the time already past is [more than] enough for doing what the [unsaved] Gentiles like to do—living [unrestrained as you have done] in a course of [shameless] sensuality, lusts, drunkenness, carousing, drinking parties, and wanton idolatries. In [connection with] all this, they [the unbelievers] are resentful and surprised that you do not [think like them, value their values and] run

[hand in hand] with them into the same excesses of dissipation and immoral freedom, and they criticize and abuse and ridicule you and make fun of your values. But they will [have to] give an account to Him who is ready to judge and pass sentence on the living and the dead. (1 Peter 4:1–5 AMP)

It's no fun to have the world hate us. Life has enough problems already. Besides, sometimes we don't even need these things to make us feel discouraged. That sometimes comes from within, for no real reason. In the next chapter, we will look at that ongoing battle.

Words of Comfort

> Be strong and of good courage, do not fear nor be
> afraid of them; for the LORD your God, He is the
> One who goes with you. He will not leave you nor
> forsake you.
> (Deuteronomy 31:6)

I'm not sure if a slap in the face works for those who
are overcome with fear. But it certainly does work in the
movies. This verse is a loving slap in the face. It's telling us
to muster strength and good courage. It's saying "Pull yourself together!" Don't fall apart in the face of fear. It's up to
us to find courage, and the slap on the face reminds us that
God is with us. Meditate on that. What more do we need?

CHAPTER FOURTEEN

THE BATTLE OF DISCOURAGEMENT

Whenever we become actively involved in any evangelistic endeavor, we must prepare our hearts to be involved in a spiritual battle. This happened to Jesus in his hour of temptation—when Satan made a personal appearance to try to kill him (see Matthew 4:6). He then had a spiritual battle on his hands from his first public sermon, when his hearers tried to kill him (see Luke 4:28–30). But Jesus was *never* discouraged. Not even in the garden of Gethsemane when fear of his immediate future caused him to sweat drops of blood. He held onto his courage (see Luke 22:44).

We, too, will have to guard ourselves against what would seem to be the number one fiery dart of the enemy—discouragement. Of course, he has an arsenal of weapons (lust, bitterness, jealousy, etc.), but if he can get rid of our courage, he wins the battle. A dis*couraged* soldier has lost effectiveness. He must continually believe in the cause for which he fights, and that conviction must drive his courage.

Early in May of 2020, I went to Huntington Beach in Southern California to get footage for our YouTube channel. The coronavirus had restricted my evangelism for a time—until I realized that I could still interview people if I set a microphone on a stand six feet from me. So I took two microphones, two microphone stands, two tripods, and two iPhones along with a large sign that invited people to do an interview.

The day in question was a Saturday. I took my dog, Sam (who wears sunglasses), drove the twenty miles from our home, and set up in an area opposite where I normally preached. This was because there were at least two dozen police officers in that area. They were obviously expecting some sort of trouble with protesters against the coronavirus confinement. I, therefore, had decided to film across the road.

I set up two microphone stands, along with the two microphones, the two tripods, and two iPhones. It was quite an ordeal adjusting the tripods, framing, and setting the iPhones, but after some time, I was ready to begin. It was then that I was told that the large area in which I had set up on was private property owned by a store. So I moved to the sidewalk.

The first man I interviewed was a Christian with an amazing testimony. However, as he spoke, cars going by the demonstrators (who had gathered with their many signs protesting the coronavirus shutdown) honked in support. After a few minutes, I found that the honking was too long and loud, so I packed up all my gear and went home.

The next day after online church, I returned to the area and set up in the same place. I engaged one gentleman in an interview, who, I began to see, was a little mentally challenged. I couldn't hear him because of the noise of the traffic, and when I asked him to speak up, he ignored me. I repeated my request, to which he said, "You can hear me." But I couldn't. Then he said it again. So I gave him a couple of gift cards and quickly ended the conversation, something I'd never done before. As he walked away, it was a little dis-couraging. Then I engaged a man in his early twenties who thought that he was God. That's because he thought that *everyone* was a god.

Suddenly, a gentleman came out of the store and said that I couldn't set my gear up on the sidewalk. I politely informed him that someone from his store the previous day had said that I was okay to set up on the sidewalk. But this man said, "I'm asking you to move." So, in wanting to be at peace with all men, I said that I'd move across the road to where there were fewer people. So I grabbed my two micro-phones, the iPhones, disassembled my two tripods, and the microphone stands, took my dog and sign, moved across, and set up in a new area.

Over the next hour, I must have pleaded with at least fifty people, but no one would come on camera. I would ask, "Excuse me. Do you think there's an afterlife?" One man told me that there was, saying that he knew so because he was a Christian. Then, for some reason he became angry with me and walked away. It was very strange. One other man stopped, saying he was a Christian and that he was familiar with my ministry. Then he began to try to argue about doctrine. I politely told him that I was busy trying to find someone to come on camera and ended the conversation. About fifty feet away I could see a man doing tae kwon do.

Suddenly, I saw a gentleman and a woman walking toward me with a small dog. To my delight, he wanted to come on camera. I was doubly delighted because I had just prayed, *Lord, please bring someone to me. I'm going to be discouraged today if I go home without an interview.*

The man's name was Nick. And as soon as I started the interview, Mr. Tae kwon do came over and stood about four feet away. At the same time, my dog (who had seen at least one hundred other dogs that day) suddenly decided to go crazy about Nick's dog. I grabbed the leash, tied it around my leg, and continued to share the gospel with Nick as Sam continued to pull on the leash.

Nick was incredibly open to the gospel. No matter what I said to him, he was in agreement. I talked about the exclusivity of Jesus—that he was the only way to God. That didn't worry him. When I came to the gospel, he was like a dying man in a desert, suddenly finding an oasis of water. When I asked him if he was ready to repent and ask for God to forgive him, he immediately bowed his head and cried out to God for mercy.

I was so pleased that I had been stubborn in battle despite all the roadblocks I had encountered. Look at this famous verse: "Therefore, my beloved brethren, be steadfast, immovable, always abounding in the work of the Lord, knowing that your labor is not in vain in the Lord" (1 Corinthians 15:58). Notice it begins with the conjunction "Therefore." The preceding verses tell us *why* we must be stubbornly steadfast and immovable:

> Now this I say, brethren, that flesh and blood cannot inherit the kingdom of God; nor does corruption inherit incorruption. Behold, I tell you a mystery: We shall not all sleep, but we shall all be changed— in a moment, in the twinkling of an eye, at the last trumpet. For the trumpet will sound, and the dead will be raised incorruptible, and we shall be changed. For this corruptible must put on incorruption, and this mortal must put on immortality. So when this corruptible has put on incorruption, and this mortal has put on immortality, then shall be brought to pass the saying that is written: "Death is swallowed up in victory."

"O Death, where is your sting?

O Hades, where is your victory?"

The sting of death is sin, and the strength of sin is the law. But thanks be to God, who gives us the victory through our Lord Jesus Christ. (1 Corinthians 15:50–57)

WORDS OF COMFORT

> Thus God, determining to show more abundantly to
> the heirs of promise the immutability of His coun-
> sel, confirmed it by an oath, that by two immutable
> things, in which it is impossible for God to lie, we
> might have strong consolation, who have fled for
> refuge to lay hold of the hope set before us.
> (Hebrews 6:17–18)

Every promise of God stands on one biblical foundation.
If that can crumble, so does our hope of everlasting life.
That foundation is the truth that it's impossible for God to
lie (see Hebrews 6:18). Lying is so against the holy nature
of our Creator that the Scriptures draw on the strength of
the word *impossible*. That means these "exceedingly great
and precious promises" (2 Peter 1:4) can be completely and
undoubtably trusted. He is faithful who promised (see Hebrews 10:23). If I don't believe that, I have nothing. Nothing
but fear in the face of impending death.

> O my Father, thank you for the precious cross. Thank
> you for the love that Jesus showed toward me, a
> wretched sinner. I believe your promises with all of
> my heart. I trust in your mercy alone, and when death
> comes it *cannot* touch me because I belong to you.
> And now I pray for this precious person reading
> these words. May you take away all fear and replace it

with your love because perfect love casts out all fear. And then cause our hearts to be turned toward those still sitting in the shadow of death, still haunted by its fear. Give us the love and the courage to tell them that Jesus Christ has abolished death and brought life and immortality to light through the gospel.

ROSE

A rose that grows and blossoms and blooms
And gives us the fragrance of sweet perfumes
With leaflets and petals, in beauty adorned
Must one day wither and wilt and be mourned
The thorns of the curse from Eden have spread
Death was inflicted, so blood must be shed
The Rose of Sharon with thorns on His head
Hung on the cross of Calvary and bled
Dying for all, as He willfully chose
So those who believe, can rise as He rose

By Emeal ("E.Z.") Zwayne

MORE PROMISES ABOUT FEAR

Memorize these and quote them aloud when fear seeks to inhabit your heart. When Jesus was attacked by Satan, he responded by quoting the Word of God. Imitate him.

> The fear of man brings a snare,
> But whoever trusts in the LORD shall be safe.
> Proverbs 29:25

> The LORD is my light and my salvation;
> Whom shall I fear?
> The LORD is the strength of my life;
> Of whom shall I be afraid?
> Psalm 27:1

> Be strong and of good courage,
> do not fear nor be afraid of them;
> for the LORD your God,
> He is the One who goes with you.
> He will not leave you nor forsake you.
> Deuteronomy 31:6

For I, the LORD your God,
will hold your right hand,
Saying to you, "Fear not, I will help you."
Isaiah 41:13

The LORD is on my side;
I will not fear.
What can man do to me?
Psalm 118:6

I sought the LORD, and He heard me,
And delivered me from all my fears.
Psalm 34:4

And the LORD, He is the One who goes before you.
He will be with you, He will not leave you nor
forsake you; do not fear nor be dismayed.
Deuteronomy 31:8

Let not your heart be troubled;
you believe in God, believe also in Me.
John 14:1

For you did not receive the spirit of bondage again
to fear, but you received the Spirit of adoption by
whom we cry out, "Abba, Father."
Romans 8:15

So we may boldly say:
"The Lord is my helper;
I will not fear.
What can man do to me?"
Hebrews 13:6

And when they saw Him walking on the sea,
they supposed it was a ghost, and cried out;
for they all saw Him and were troubled.
But immediately He talked with them and said to
them, "Be of good cheer! It is I; do not be afraid."
Mark 6:49–50

But even if you should suffer for righteousness'
sake, you are blessed. "And do not be afraid of
their threats, nor be troubled."
1 Peter 3:14

In God (I will praise His word),
In God I have put my trust;
I will not fear.
What can flesh do to me?
Psalm 56:4

As a father pities his children,
So the Lord pities those who fear Him.
Psalm 103:13

Then the angel said to her, "Do not be afraid,
Mary, for you have found favor with God. And
behold, you will conceive in your womb and bring
forth a Son, and shall call His name Jesus."

Luke 1:30–31

But when Jesus heard it,
He answered him, saying,
"Do not be afraid; only believe,
and she will be made well."

Luke 8:50

Are not five sparrows sold for two copper coins?
And not one of them is forgotten before God.
But the very hairs of your head are all numbered.
Do not fear therefore; you are of more value than
many sparrows.

Luke 12:6–7

Then the angel said to them, "Do not be afraid, for
behold, I bring you good tidings of great joy which
will be to all people."

Luke 2:10

Though an army may encamp against me,
My heart shall not fear;
Though war may rise against me,
In this I will be confident.

Psalm 27:3

ABOUT THE AUTHOR

Ray Comfort is the best-selling author of more than one hundred books. He is the cohost of an award-winning television program that airs in 190 countries and the producer of award-winning movies that have been viewed by millions (see www.FullyFreeFilms.com). He lives in Southern California with his wife, Sue, and has three grown children. For more information, visit LivingWaters.com.